AS I WAS SAYING

Recollections and Miscellaneous Essays

V O L U M E   O N E
T E X A S ,   P R E - T E X A S ,   C A M B R I D G E

Colin Rowe

edited by Alexander Caragonne

The MIT Press   Cambridge, Massachusetts   London, England

This book was set in Garamond 3 by Graphic Composition, Inc., and was printed and bound in the United States of America.

Library of Congress Cataloging-in-Publication Data

Rowe, Colin.

    As I was saying : recollections and miscellaneous essays / Colin Rowe ; edited by Alexander Caragonne.

       p.   cm.

    Includes bibliographical references and index.

    Contents: v. 1. Texas, pre-Texas, Cambridge.

    ISBN 0-262-18167-3 (hc : alk. paper)

    1. Architecture—Philosophy.   2. Architecture—Aesthetics.

I. Caragonne, Alexander.   II. Title.

NA2500.R74   1995

720′.1—dc20   95-15191

                                                            CIP

Contents

Editor's Note   ix

Introduction   1

Two Italian Encounters   3

Henry-Russell Hitchcock   11

Texas and Mrs. Harris   25

Comments of Harwell Hamilton Harris to the Faculty,
May 25, 1954   41

Lockhart, Texas   55

Transparency: Literal and Phenomenal, Part II   73

Review: *Forms and Functions of Twentieth Century Architecture*
by Talbot Hamlin   107

Review: *Roots of Contemporary American Architecture*
by Lewis Mumford   123

Cambridge 1958–1962   131

Le Corbusier: Utopian Architect   135

The Blenheim of the Welfare State   143

A Vote of Thanks   153

Review: Student Work of the Architectural Association   159

Review: *A Testament* by Frank Lloyd Wright   167

Review: *Architecture: Nineteenth and Twentieth Centuries*
by Henry-Russell Hitchcock   177

Sidgwick Avenue   185

Index of Names   195

Editor's Note

Almost thirty years ago, the eminent British architectural historian and writer Reyner Banham, nearing the end of a perfunctory review of *British Buildings, 1960–1964,* launched into what can only be described as a hysterical outburst:

> But perhaps the most baffling aspect of the book to the lay reader will be its dedication. *Who is Colin Rowe?* you will ask. He is in fact the most in-group of all the groupy people represented here; the only living British critic or architecture pundit to become not only the object of a secret-type cult, but also an anti-cult. Rowe's writings of the forties and fifties affected most of the in-group deeply and permanently (and myself as well, I freely admit).[1]

And, he continued,

> If the in-group have their way; and Rowe is seriously put
> forward as the next principal of the Architectural Associa-
> tion School, he will find an underground opposition move-
> ment waiting for him. For one fact remains inescapable: in
> spite of the very high quality indeed of the best buildings
> illustrated here, the selection is narrow, prejudiced, and
> represents only a very small slice of the lively work going
> forward in Britain at present, and there is a younger genera-
> tion of architects coming on who are determined that the
> in-group shall not become a new establishment with Rowe
> as its *éminence grise*.[2]

Thus it was that Banham (a latter-day Salieri to Rowe's
mini-Mozart?) introduced Colin Rowe in his now well-known role
as *éminence grise,* a role that Tom Wolfe also assigned him over a de-
cade later in *From Bauhaus to Our House,* as the Machiavellian presence behind yet another in-group: the New York Five.

Banham's and Wolfe's recognition of Rowe's powerful influence, however superficial, was at least well founded. From his
first arrival on the scene in the late 1940s Rowe has commanded the
attention of succeeding generations of young architects. He has,
however (despite Banham's wholly gratuitous caveat), remained
quite outside *any* architectural establishment and from his remote
Ithaca address for nearly thirty years has quite simply devoted himself to his students and his writing. As to *organizing* an opposition,
it is safe to say that Rowe has carefully demurred. Subscribing, no
doubt, to Groucho Marx's declaration that he would never join any
club that would invite him to be a member, the quality of Rowe's
imaginary architectural *salon des refusés* has always been founded
upon attitudes that resist categorization and defy slogans. A dialec-
tician with an avowed mistrust of an overt Hegelian metaphysic, a
connoisseur of transparent Analytical Cubism and the *gravitas* of

Empire furniture, an afficionado of Italo-Texas landscapes, an adopted American with a fondness for the unreconstructed Southern rebel, Rowe has continued to provide a valuable, intellectually respectable alternative to the prevailing (and persistent) architectural posturing of the day. Indeed, his own posture might be viewed as a counter-*dimostrazione* of sorts. As such, Rowe has employed his considerable intellectual stamina and moral passion in a struggle to understand the unexamined beliefs that support the superstructure of our twentieth-century architectural culture.

In the early 1950s Rowe's earliest intimations of Modern architecture's polemical contradictions emerged—that late-Victorian marriage of French rationalism and German metaphysics that provided the intellectual basis for Modernism's rapid postwar ascension in Europe and America. Confronted with its later issue, those noisy, quarrelsome, avant-garde offspring that have appeared in succeeding decades—New Brutalism, Superstudio, Archigram, Architettura Razionale, Conceptual architecture, Postmodernism, and lately Deconstructivism—Rowe has persuasively advocated a consistently critical examination. On the one hand genuinely fascinated by the formal, spatial implications of "that revolutionary constellation of novelties"[3] that presented themselves as the emblems of a new architecture almost a century ago, but also deeply skeptical of the positivist, chiliastic program for society that the new architecture was supposed to foreshadow, Rowe has devoted a large part of his writings to disentangling one from the other.

Back in 1947, a now legendary essay[4] that first drew attention to the conceptual similarities of the villas Malcontenta and Garches revealed Rowe's powers of observation and incomparable eye to a happy few. Since then, despite a steady though oddly unacknowledged production of work, Rowe's mythical, guru status seems to have grown in inverse proportion to his perceived output. Part of this is no doubt due to his distaste for self-promotion—a Warburgian devotion to the pursuit of ideas rather than notoriety—and part to a certain satisfaction with the surreptitious circulation of his work via a network of students, colleagues, friends, and

Editor's Note

admirers, which he himself acknowledged in his prefatory remarks to *Mathematics of the Ideal Villa and Other Essays.*[5]

The current collection includes articles, essays, eulogies, lectures, reviews, and memoranda, some of which have appeared only in obscure periodicals (obscure at least to American audiences) over the past fifty years. Many have never been published at all. Also included is a retrospective view of selected work of the Urban Design Studio at Cornell and of related projects by Rowe and his associates and colleagues. The three volumes group Rowe's work more or less chronologically: *Texas, Pre-Texas, Cambridge* comprises items written during his first extended introduction to the United States (1951–1958), prior to and during his tenure at the University of Texas in Austin, concluding with those written while at Cambridge University from 1958 to 1962. The second volume, *Cornelliana,* contains writings prepared while teaching at Cornell University in Ithaca from 1962 until his retirement; the third, *Urbanistics* deals primarily with urban design.

Each volume, though self-contained, is part of an ensemble or tapestry in which several related topics interwoven. With the denouement of Modern architecture always present as a recurring theme, Rowe's expositions on the education of young architects, urban design, historical precedent, technology, context and invention, style, and ideas versus talent provide a fascinating record of the prodigious, thoroughly original train of thought of one of this century's greatest architectural teachers, writers, and critics.

Notes

1. Reyner Banham in *New Society,* March 17, 1966, reviewing Douglas Stephen, Kenneth Frampton, and Michael Carapetian, *British Buildings, 1960–1964* (London: A. & C. Black, 1965).

2. Indeed Rowe was put forward as a candidate for the school at the AA in 1966. Possibly Banham's not so subtle threat to lead the opposition against Rowe was a factor in the final judgment of the selection committee not to select him.

3. Colin Rowe, "Architectural Education in the USA: Issues, Ideas and People," *Lotus International,* no. 27 (1980).

4. Colin Rowe, "The Mathematics of the Ideal Villa," *Architectural Review* (March 1947).

5. Rowe declared, "Had it not been for inertia this particular collection might well have been published in the early sixties; but, while I sometimes regret that this was not done, I am by no means dismayed by the delay. For most of these essays have remained, in some degree, relevant and some of them have long enjoyed a piratical, xeroxed, student circulation which, to me, can only be gratifying." Rowe, *The Mathematics of the Ideal Villa and Other Essays* (Cambridge: MIT Press, 1976), vii.

AS I WAS SAYING

Introduction

This collection of essays, memoranda, *disjecta membra,* and memorabilia for the most part unpublished—or published in somewhat reclusive and inaccessible sources—extends as far back as 1953, and its putting together has been suggested—perhaps better to say imposed upon my reluctance—by my friends Alexander Caragonne and Roger Conover of the MIT Press; and so, I have succumbed to their insistence. Indeed, without it I am pretty sure that the topics here discussed would never have been either resurrected or represented.

But by what criteria should all this *matériel* be organized?

Apparently, as even myself can perceive, there is some sort of thematic persistence which prevails throughout most of what follows; but I hesitate—it would only confuse the reader—to impose a simple classification by category. The temporal, chronological problem excludes this possibility; as a result I find myself reluctantly obliged to introduce some autobiographical component.

And, therefore, let us now so proceed.

The two and a half years (five academic semesters) which I spent at the University of Texas in Austin, 1954–1956, constitute something of a watershed—or even an epiphany—in my life. But just how—by what freak of fortune or misfortune—did myself arrive in Texas?

I had received my architectural education at the University of Liverpool during the years 1938–1942 and 1944–1945; and it is from this connection that I derive two of my greatest friends, the late James Stirling and Robert Maxwell, until recently the dean of architecture at Princeton University. I spent the years 1942–1944 (or part of them) in a not very remarkable military service which was terminated, very effectively, on the occasion of my eighteenth parachute jump, by a fractured spine.

In some ways this was fortuitous, since most of those with whom I trained were killed in the Sicily landings and there was always Normandy to follow; but, in other ways, it was less than agreeable. A fractured spine, with some residual paraplegia in the left leg—and this was easily to be excited—rendered leaning over a drafting board the reverse of easy. Consequently, an invitation from the Warburg Institute at the University of London to accept a junior fellowship could only be an attractive proposition.

So it was thus that I became an architect manqué; the result was my working for two years as, at that time, Rudolf Wittkower's only student on the preparation of a thesis, "The Theoretical Drawings of Inigo Jones," which, apparently, was just what those Warburgians wished to receive. Not only Rudy Wittkower but Fritz Saxl and Gertrude Bing were highly impressed by it; if I thought they were deluded, just possibly I might have been wrong.

Anyway, in this period begins the series of my interminable trips to Italy, and about two of these I append memoranda written to myself in 1988.

Two Italian Encounters

Written 1988

We had been awakened in the morning at Chambéry by the usual French noise to be associated with the Fourteenth of July (this was in 1947); and quickly we put ourselves in the train for Turin. But would you believe it? Getting to Turin took almost all day, and we only arrived there in the late afternoon. Then we took another train to Rome, again very slow. Such had been the destruction of Italian communications that we arrived at Genoa only about midnight; and, of course, at Genoa what I, in those days, thought to be all the riffraff of the Mediterranean proletariat came in to crowd the situation. And thence on we labored, in what seemed to have become a traveling slum, through all of those tunnels throughout all of that night, to arrive at Pisa at about five in the morning, and at Pisa all the Genovese workmen got out. But for us, in spite of this relief, we were compelled to go on and on. And so we still labored through Livorno and Grosseto and Civitavecchia slowly over all of those tempo-

4

rary Bailey bridges, slowly, slowly, to arrive at Rome only about five o'clock in the afternoon. A journey of about thirty-two hours between Chambéry and Rome!

There then occurred a period of three weeks in Rome in which, obsessed with early Christian churches, I seem to remember that my Canadian traveling companion, Sydney Key, insisted that we see at least three before breakfast each morning. But was this insistence on early Christian churches a good idea? On the whole, I really think that it was, and this because, quite simply, on subsequent visits to Rome I have known where all of these churches happen to be so that as long as I live I shall never wish to see another. Le Corbusier might have been crazed for Santa Maria in Cosmedin—but, as for myself, I can get along perfectly well without it.

Anyway, it was after three weeks that we left, this time in a bus, for Siena; and I will now try to recapture my first experience of the Via Cassia which, since then, I have driven on so many occasions. Since those days it has degenerated. Since then there have been too many interventions made by highway engineers, too much cutting into hills and filling in of declivities, so that, for great stretches of this road, the intimate contact, the empathy with landscape which was once sponsored by its rollings and twistings is no longer to be enjoyed. But, in 1947, driving along this road—even in a bus—was almost a visual equivalent to the rhythm of Mendelssohn's Italian Symphony—ta *ra* ra, ta *ra* ra, ta *raa* di ra ra—which I am convinced was derived from a north-south drive along this selfsame road; and this is to partly explain the immense excitement which I felt—and still feel—in approaching such towns as Sutri and Capranica, though not so much so at Montefiascone and very grim Radicofani, isolated up there on its hill and now, because of a bypass, very little visited.

All of this a protracted prelude to the experience which was awaiting me in Florence at the Pensione Annalena in the Via Porta Romana, where we sat down to dinner and were very quickly joined by a distinctly angular lady who introduced herself, rather improbably I couldn't help thinking, as Libby Tannenbaum working for some art magazine in New York and even to me—at least I knew that much—recognizable as coming from Brooklyn. But, if this was not exactly a meeting of the minds, it was amusing for me because between Syd and Libby there developed a conversation from which I was completely excluded. While I wanted to talk about landscape, they wanted to talk about the attribution of late medieval pictures: Was Richard Orfner right in assigning Such-and-Such in So-and-So to Taddeo Gaddi or should it be Bernardo Daddi? Simply, my mind was just rocking under the impact of all this erudition; and, though I didn't care then and don't care now whoever it might have been—in this phase of history—who did what and where, I felt myself reduced to utter insignificance. If this is a typical encounter of persons from the North American continent, then how very odd North America must be.

Meanwhile, across the room there was sitting another very obvious American. Distinctly saturnine and evidently the product of some privileged Eastern school, though I wasn't quite able to read the information which his appearance conveyed, he was equipped with the inevitable seersucker suit and crew cut of those postwar years; and after we had adjourned after dinner to the portico, it was perhaps to be expected that he would join us. This was Craig Smyth, later chairman of art history at New York University and, still later, director of the Harvard Center for Renaissance Studies at the Villa I Tatti outside Settignano but, at present, sent over by the Frick Collection to form opinions about Andrea del Castagno in connection with the authenticity of a picture which the Frick had under consideration.

As he came to join us, one wondered had he felt a little bit lonely sitting over there all by himself? Or had he been curious about an English-speaking group of three of which one member was so strangely silent while the other two were emphatically not? Myself only knows that, with his arrival, the noise level and the vehemence of the conversation increased and that while, even then, I could have said something about Andrea del Castagno, for the most part I became astonished by the acrimonious argument. It was perplexing. By my not so simple English standards these persons were all so *rough* with one another; and, of course, the English, before they will condescend to argument, will always resort to superciliousness. But nothing supercilious here, and it didn't seem to relate to the rules of the game. No, in their own way these persons were ruthless, to each other they conceded nothing, they made no attempt to massage each other's amour propre; and, disconcerted though I may have been, at least I was obliged to recognize a social situation which compelled exploration.

Then, it was three years later that I came to enjoy another American exposure which was much more entertaining and pleasurable.

Toward the end of August in 1950, in the Church of San Francesco at Arezzo, I was introduced (or more probably presented) to Mrs. Arthur Brown, Jr., of Burlingame, California; and it was an occasion that I vividly remember. Indeed it was almost a minor Henry James event. Quite abruptly, the frescoes of Piero della Francesca vanished; Solomon and the Queen of Sheba, Constantine and the Empress Helena were all eclipsed; and Mrs. Brown, sinking into a chair, proceeded to become very much her own version of a grande dame holding court.

"So where," she said, "are you goin' from here? What, Montepulciano and Pienza? Well, now, jus' think about that! Well, like minds do think alike 'cause that's just where we're goin'. Well, y'all had just better come to lunch with Arturo and the gals 'cause they'd all just love to meet you."

Mrs. Brown came from Louisiana and possessed a certain unreconstructed Southern *folie de grandeur* (almost she lived with her lorgnette); and 'Arturo', wearing a nice blue blazer with the little red pin of the Légion d'Honneur, was very slowly divulged to be a quasi-friend of Piacentini; the architect, in and around San Francisco, of the City Hall, the Opera House, the Veteran's Building, the Coit Memorial Tower, of miscellaneous palaces for the Crockers,

and of very much else including, in Washington, D.C., the better
part of the Federal Triangle. But, as for me, as I entered the Buca di
San Francesco—then, I think, a very much better restaurant than it
now is—I had no knowledge of all this. Simply, I had received intimations of some mid–West Coast survival of the belle époque; and
two days later, as we drove from Perugia through the *creta senese*, I remember feeling that my intimations had been amply rewarded.

For there were the feminine voices which said all sorts of
things. There were the cultural voices: "Why I guess we're so *intime*
with Pio Secondo by now that we kinda' think he'd be offended if
we missed out on his birthplace. Why, ever since I read the first
lines by Poliziano I've been just dying to go to Montepulciano";
and then there was the social voice—Mrs. Brown, otherwise known
as Jasmine, and very serious: "Well I gotta remind you. You just got
to think about So-and-So from Burlingame. Well she married, don't
you know, a Prince Doria. But then, you know, she was never quite
accepted in Roman society. So, home in Burlingame, we always
called her the Princess Back-Doria."

So with the background of splendid landscapes and the foreground of conversations more or less remembered of long ago, there
is my witness to Arturo's fatigue. For Arturo was mostly interested
in visuals, and the great names of culture and society were not
likely to make him highly animated. At Montepulciano, I recollect
that San Biagio made him happy; and, at San Biagio, the *presbiterio*
made his wife overjoyed ("Why Arturo, this is jus' the little house
that I want down at Pebble Beach"). And was it strange that nobody seemed to know that the priest's house at San Biagio had already been 'used up' for the courtyard of the Fogg Museum at
Harvard? On the whole I don't really think that it was; but, as I
think about Arthur Brown at Montepulciano, I am made increasingly aware of an intellectual generosity which was very grand and
of a physical presence which defied his age. For lunch we sat upon a
terrace. In a provincial Italian way it was both sublime and casual.
The views were extensive, the local furniture seemed to be adequate. Also, it is a terrace which I can never rediscover; but then, as

Two Italian Encounters

we sat upon this terrace and Arturo was, at last, allowed his say, I became equipped to hear something of his story.

About the year 1900, at the Ecole des Beaux-Arts, Arthur Brown had been a student of Gromort. He had been there at approximately the same time as Julia Morgan, and, as I have since been told, in San Francisco there had been rumors which linked the two names. However, be this as it may, to return to the Arthur Brown whom I knew. He had never been in London—and was pleased and proud to say it—since a few days before the coronation of Edward VII; and he had never wished to go there again. But all the same, in Rome—and this was apostolic succession stuff—he was determined to take me to Santa Maria in Campitelli—"In my days, in Gromort's studio there was a real *culte* for Rainaldi."

Of course, I was more than highly surprised. For what, I thought, could Carlo Rainaldi have to do with the Ecole des Beaux-Arts? And wasn't Santa Maria in Campitelli (to quote Rudolf Wittkower) "that extraordinary building [where] North Italian planning is coupled with Roman gravity and Mannerist retrogressions turned into progressive tendencies," was it not really a fairly recent discovery of German art history? Which was how I felt. But dutifully (and perhaps with a certain innocent, intellectual condescension), I expressed none of my crude surprise to Arturo. Indeed I dissimulated any serious knowledge of the church, which I had visited on two previous occasions but which I still knew best from Wittkower's remarkable article, "Carlo Rainaldi and the Architecture of the High Baroque in Rome."

And so we parted in Perugia where the Browns, needless to say, were staying at the Albergo Brufani. They had come down from Paris in two hired cars, one for themselves and one for the luggage—not exactly the style of the period; and in this same style, they were going on to Naples because Arturo was concerned that his daughters should enjoy a quick look—"I just gotta take the gals down to the Cappucini at Amalfi and then I gotta show them the *coup d'oeil* from Capodimonte"—so that it was not until about a week later that we all came to meet again in Rome.

It was thus one morning toward mid-September that we proceeded to pay our respects to Carlo Rainaldi, emerging, Arthur Brown from the Hassler and myself from what was then the cheap Pensione Pfister across the street (where Miss Pfister, intensely Swiss, kept tortoises on the roof, one of them *un piccolo americano,* and where the cats extracted enjoyment from turning them upside down). And, from Piazza della Trinità dei Monti we took a short taxi ride to Santa Maria in Campitelli, where very quickly I found myself in the presence of a great connoisseur.

"Why you just gotta see that this is related to Vanbrugh, but he is a bit too *mesquin* for me. But the management of the *dégagements* and the manipulation of the light! You just gotta see all this!"; and, as excitement mounted, then we could only go on to the Chiesa Nuova and Borromini's Oratorio dei Filippini next door, where the excitement became strenuous. "Well, in Gromort's studio, we perfectly understood how successful Borromini was with his *hors d'échelles"*—an *hors d'échelle* apparently being the calculated intrusion of an out-of-scale element.

So need I say that though there was much else that occurred in that September in Rome—including the beatification of the Blessed Maria Goretti, when I succeeded in getting us out of St. Peter's by the use of Mrs. Brown's hat pin as a sort of bayonet (a strategy to be recommended)—it was still Rainaldi and Borromini as seen by Arthur Brown which provided the high point. For, first of all, there had been disclosed a condition of sensibility entirely remote from anything which I had been led to associate with either California or San Francisco and, secondly, I had made acquaintance with at least one particular French studio language of some fifty years back which was very different from the art historical language to which I had lately been exposed.

But, of course, these two languages must, almost always, be quite independent of each other. The studio language, which belongs to the process of architectural education as it relates to the drawing board, is, of necessity, the voice of immediacy and enthusiasm. It is the voice of excited critics and intelligent students who may, all of them, be largely ignorant; and one may know quite a few of its variants as they exist at the present day. But the art historical language is something other. It is the voice of caution and aspires to erudition; and if the studio language, always vivacious, is prone to be the language of uncriticized tradition, then the art historical language, often still attempting to realize that impossible ideal of Ranke's, simply to show it how it really was (*wie es eigentlich gewesen*), will always operate to separate and divide, will always insist that, in Paris and in 1900, there could never be any appraisal of Santa Maria in Campitelli and, absolutely, no access to the Oratorio dei Filippini. And it was the total of all these intuitions which I acquired from Arthur Brown as we walked around Carlo Rainaldi's beautiful church.

A long parenthesis. But, all the same, when I reported my experience with Arthur Brown to Rudolf Wittkower back in London, I *did* know exactly how he would react. Understandably, he had a proprietary interest in Rainaldi and it was scarcely to be tolerated that the same interest (and long antecedent to his own) had been expressed by an architect so notoriously *retardataire* as Arthur Brown. No, I *must* be *wrong*. My evidence *must* be invalid. I was the victim of an hallucination or, if not, I was the engineer of an elaborate and not very amusing joke. No, in Paris and in 1900, there *can* be *no* way and just you forget it!

So, knowing Wittkower in these moods, I didn't persist; but, all the same, it was from that day with Arthur Brown that I began to feel the need for a direct experience of the United States. There had been the art historical confrontation in Florence and there had followed the architectural revelation in Rome. But, surely, all Americans could not be like those whom I had met in Italy? This seemed quite contrary to the intuitions of common sense and to the received 'wisdom' of England that: Americans just don't talk like this, and what, in the end, *is* it that they know *anyway?*

Nevertheless it was only a year later that I removed myself to the U.S., which, to me at that time, meant I removed myself to study at Yale with Henry-Russell Hitchcock.

TEXAS, PRE-TEXAS, CAMBRIDGE

Henry-Russell Hitchcock

Written 1988

Said Philip Johnson one day: "Oh, if only Russell had the gift of clarity and if only Nikolaus had an eye." Said Sybil Moholoy-Nagy slightly later: "Well, if Pevsner is the telephone book of architecture, then surely Hitchcock must be the yellow pages." Wrote Bernard Berenson in August 1955: "Hitchcock, whom I recall as a rather rotund and unattractive young man, appeared yesterday, transformed into a breezy, middle-aged, full but not loud voiced, Viking-type of American. It is the type I fall for regardless of attainments and achievements because I find them life-enhancing."[1]

So much for a random sampling of casual judgement; and, of course, one cannot help being arrested by the image of Hitchcock as Berenson's Platonic idea of a Bostonian pseudo-Viking. An optical illusion? But also a highly captivating and completely understandable misreading. For, as one begins to contemplate that inexorable, occasionally catastrophic conversational ebullience, that never relaxed and always brusque explosiveness of judgement ("such tenu *and* absolutely *no* looks"), that early twentieth century emphasis on minor parts of speech ("*But* she said to me *and* I said to her . . ."), that curious combination of the naughty boy and the pontifical professor, that slightly nautical flavoring of Edward VII (or is it Sir Thomas Beecham, or Sir Thomas Lipton, or William Howard Taft?), one might easily be persuaded that the time is 1910, that the place is Cowes or Kiel, that the yacht has been brought over from Newport, and that the affable, irrepressible *viveur* will shortly be leaving to take the waters at Gastein.

But, "full but not loud voiced"! Or should one say equipped with a histrionic whisper which could penetrate every part of La Scala or Covent Garden? In any case, not to reply to a rhetorical question. Conceivably, up at Vallombrosa,[2] H.R.H. *might* have been subdued. But it is unlikely. It is unlikely that anything could inhibit that little intellectual kettle; and, therefore, from the externals of the kettle (so gratifying to the ninety-one-year-old Berenson) to its contents: in spite of Berenson, those contents were almost certainly *not* Viking—though does one really know what those old Vikings were up to in Amalfi/Ravello, Cefalù, and all those other little southern places?

So just what could those two remorseless addicts of conversation, whose interests were so divergent, have had to say to each other that August afternoon? They could scarcely have talked about painting or architecture, about which there would have been little possibility of either agreement or conflict; but, being both graduates of Harvard—though some forty years apart—it must have been toward Harvard topics that they addressed themselves, with Berenson expressing his concern that the university might still not accept his bequest of the Villa I Tatti and its collections and Hitchcock (who was distinctly deaf) attempting to listen very attentively. After which did the conversation languish? Or was the name Arthur Kingsley Porter very rapidly interjected?

Kingsley Porter, Harvard art historian, had traveled with Berenson in Greece in 1923, and it must have been about that time that the young Hitchcock became one of his students, specializing, I would guess, in Romanesque architecture and, even more improbably, in the Merovingian and Carolingian minutiae to which his attention had been directed. But, if this much I know precisely, it may also call for a very slim digression upon Harvard art history as it had gradually articulated itself.

Shortly after the mid-nineteenth century Charles Eliot Norton had received and idolized the message of Ruskin; and since the 1820s Harvard had always been accessible to the message of German idealism. Indeed, among Harvard boys to go to Germany one of the earliest must have been Hitchcock's great-grandfather (or would it have been great-great?). This is the historian George Bancroft (1800–1891), who went on to the universities of Heidelberg, Göttingen, and Berlin—this in the mid-1820s—and returned to Massachusetts to found the Round Hill School at Northampton (H.R.H. used to think of this as something wildly ironic), and all this before becoming American minister in London (1846–1849) and in Berlin (1867–1874).

However, by 1920, with Ruskinianism in full retreat and with German idealism more than slightly faded, there had come to prevail a very different critical tone. In contradistinction to these English and German influences it was French; and it is within a French orbit, the orbit of positivism and Auguste Choisy, that myself would place the somewhat unexciting contributions of Kingsley Porter, about whom I suggest that Berenson and Hitchcock talked that afternoon in August 1955.

Undoubtedly they also talked (they must have) about the circumstances of Kingsley Porter's demise. He had bought a large property in County Donegal and it was there, one day, that, very abruptly, he disappeared. Had he been drowned in the sea? Or had he been sucked into the depths of an Irish bog? Nobody seems to know; but, as far as I can understand, with his excessive attention to facts at the expense of generalizations, it must have been Kingsley Porter who had been responsible for the ultimate mental formation of the Russell Hitchcock whom I knew at Yale.

Henry-Russell Hitchcock

A case of preponderant teacher and most favored student, it was probably for these reasons that Hitchcock received a fellowship to continue his Merovingian researches in Paris (the Germanophile George Bancroft would surely have disapproved); and it was thus that he arrived in Paris, I would think in September 1926, to discover a situation which, in Boston, he never could have envisaged. For this was the Paris of the American expatriates, of Ernest Hemingway, Scott and Zelda Fitzgerald, Gertrude Stein, and Winnaretta Singer (Princesse de Polignac and sewing machine heiress); it was the Paris of Michael and Sarah Stein, of the Cooks and the Churchs and all those transatlantic clients of Le Corbusier, the Paris of Gerald and Sarah Murphy, friends of Léger—he of the Crouch and Fitzgerald store on Madison Avenue and a model for Dick Diver in *Tender Is the Night*—and both of them said to have invented the Riviera as a summer resort. But, above all, it was in this Paris, which I imagine Hitchcock to have entered with his intolerable self-assurance, that he was to meet a young American of his own generation who was totally to redirect his own life. This was Peter van der Meulen Smith, the bearer of one of those impeccably American Anglo-Dutch names.

But, apart from being an architect (in Paris he worked for André Lurçat), just who was he? He was short-lived. Hitchcock dedicated his first book, *Modern Architecture: Romanticism and Reintegration* (1929) "To the memory of Peter van der Meulen Smith," and he once told me he had gone to Berlin in connection with Smith's death—or funeral. In the 1929 book, Hitchcock published two of Smith's perspectives for a house on the Massachusetts North Shore, I imagine not too far from Swampscott or Manchester-by-the-Sea (fig. 1), and these drawings still astonish me.

They represent a project of 1927, which even by the standards of fifty years later would be outstanding but which—at that date—was entirely clairvoyant in its awareness of the most recent French and Dutch innovations. It is a project which, for me, implies the most intimate acquaintance with the early Le Corbusier proposals for the villa Les Terrasses at Garches, a project which may lead

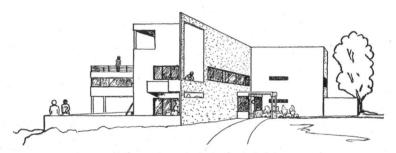

1. House for the Massachusetts North Shore, 1927. Peter van der Meulen Smith.

Henry-Russell Hitchcock

to the question: just how well did Smith know the Steins and Le Corbusier? Because, apparently being aware of early drawings for Garches, he was also able to expand upon them.

I refer to the frame/wall which extends from the main volume of the house and which serves to screen some sort of porch or belvedere: the sort of thing that Giuseppe Terragni might have done but never did? It is apparent that Peter van der Meulen Smith was intrigued by that early group of studies for Garches which has always absorbed my own attention (fig. 2). In the *Oeuvre Complète* they are dated July 20, 1926; and if one looks at the side elevation of the unbuilt Garches, one may find exactly this element which, on the North Shore, has now been elevated to a position of prominence.

A fairly well-to-do young man proposing to build for a member of his family, one might suppose Smith to have been; but, in any case, this house is a pretty breathtaking statement, and one may well understand how it was able to deflect Hitchcock from his designated pursuit of Merovingian bric-a-brac. Russell Hitchcock was apt to speak of Friedrich Gilly as "a Giorgione to Schinkel's Titian"; and, when I heard him do so, I was always rather sad because, to me, it seemed evident that he was also referring to Peter van der Meulen Smith, his own architectural Giorgione, and there was to be no American architectural Titian to follow.

It was in this way that H.R.H. abandoned all ideas of the dissertation which he was supposed to write, that he set aside a probable career as an early medievalist at Harvard, that, instead, he set out to produce, in the United States, a climate of opinion propitious to an understanding of the lesson which he had learned in Paris; and, this was the book of 1929, I think his best book and the book which brought me to study with him at Yale.

The more long-term results were, understandably, something of an estrangement from Harvard and, perhaps, a somewhat shriveled academic career at Smith College in Northampton, Massachusetts, which must have been made more acceptable by an extensive cultivation of persons at Hartford and Farmington,

Croquis 1926

2. Les Terrasses, Garches, early sketches. Le Corbusier.

Henry-Russell Hitchcock

Connecticut. At Hartford there was A. Everett ("Chick") Austin, director of the Wadsworth Atheneum from 1927 to 1945 before going on to the Ringling Museum in Sarasota, Florida, for which he bought a small eighteenth century theater from the town of Asolo; but at Hartford Austin had built himself a replica house—apparently very big but, in reality, quite small—with French, Piedmontese, and even Bauhaus rooms assembled inside it. A representative of a pseudo-*maniera,* Surrealist culture, this house is, to say the least, unexpected; and, with the slightest modifications (including stucco on brick to stucco on timber frame), it is based upon Vincenzo Scamozzi's Villa Ferretti, outside Venice, at Dolo on the Brenta Canal. About 1930 a very arcane choice but one which must have gratified the recently de-Parisianized Hitchcock otherwise lost in Northampton.

Then, at Farmington, there was James Thrall Soby with his miscellaneous Picassos. The extension to the Soby house, a fairly big living room out at the back, as far as I am aware was the only building which Hitchcock ever designed. But all this local discernment and cosmopolitanism clearly had its contacts with comparable circles in New York and this must have led, through Alfred Barr, to Philip Johnson, curator of the Museum of Modern Art's exhibition of 1932, "Modern Architecture."

To the catalogue of this exhibition Barr, Johnson, and Hitchcock all made contributions and all made reference to an architectural manifestation (otherwise "Modern architecture") known to Hitchcock and Johnson as "*an* international style" and known to Alfred Barr as "*the* International Style"; Barr's use of this term was quite excessive. In his foreword of about one thousand words, as far as I am able to count, he refers to "the International Style" on at least ten occasions—or once every one hundred words—so that this usage came to usurp the official title of the exhibition, at least in the popular consciousness and for the purposes of journalistic headlines.

But an unfortunate pseudo-title this surely was and increasingly became; for although the new architecture certainly presented a new style, this was *not* what its exponents wished to hear; and, as for any idea of internationalism, at that date this was distinctly intolerable to American isolationists, chauvinists, and would-be regionalists. So was this all a case of polemics or bad public relations? No doubt it was a bit of both. All the same, what was intended was very far removed from what was *thought* to be intended. It was no recommendation or directive for an internationalization of architecture; rather it was a statement that an internationalization of architecture already existed. In fact it was a title derived from previous art historical formulations, like the term International Gothic, which had lately been introduced as a designation for certain late-medieval manifestations.

The inadequacies of the concept of an International Style, as promoted by Russell Hitchcock and Philip Johnson, should not require extended notice. Briefly, Hitchcock and Johnson conceived of a modern architecture without irrational motivations. They did not labor to explore the not-so-unconscious mind of the modern architect in continental Europe. They were not anxious to expose all that mishmash of millennialistic illusions, chiliastic excitements, and quasi-Marxist fantasies; and, if I may quote myself:

> It was thus, and either by inadvertence or design, that when in the nineteen Thirties, European modern architecture came to infiltrate the United States, it was introduced as simply a new approach to building—and not much more. That is, it was introduced, largely purged of its ideological or societal content; and it became available, not as an evident manifestation or cause of socialism, but rather as a *décor de la vie* for Greenwich, Connecticut or as a suitable veneer for the corporate activities of enlightened capitalism.[3]

Inadvertence or design? But even supposing that Russell and Philip had any very developed interest in the strangely involuted psychology of the modern architect, in what expurgated form

Henry-Russell Hitchcock

could they have presented his products? For, after all, their sponsor just did happen to be the Museum of Modern Art, at a later date to be known to Le Corbusier as *la Fondation Rockefeller* ("je m'en fiche de la Fondation Rockefeller"). Nevertheless, their contentions and persuasions certainly came to prevail; and, if these became fashionable rather than acceptable, within a very few years they had created a state of mind, a state of mind made evident by the 1937 appointment of Walter Gropius as chairman (not dean) of the Graduate School of Design at Harvard.

On one occasion in London I remember a lunch with Hitchcock at a small restaurant in the King's Road, Chelsea. It was at the north end of Paulton's Square; it had been designed by Oliver Hill and where it used to be there is now an expensive antique shop—to which, incidentally, Jim Stirling was in the habit of selling off pieces of furniture which no longer absorbed his interest. But, in this restaurant, Hitchcock was vociferating with all the acoustic insensitivity of the deaf. In other words, he was broadcasting quite gratuitous information to all and sundry and the substance of his information was that "in this restaurant and at this very table I gave lunch to Jimmy Conant just before he went away to offer the job to Walter Gropius"—opportunity for surprise and acclaim.

But, if I can perfectly well see James Bryant Conant, then president of Harvard, leaving the restaurant, turning left and then left again into Church Street to the second modern house on the right—Gropius and Fry—in order to make the Harvard offer, I still don't know how to interpret this. That there had been privy discussions within a restricted circle must be apparent, as it must be further apparent that Hitchcock, if he had not participated in them, must have been entirely cognizant of their subject. But what was this politics all about? And, although I can only confess my ignorance, I do know that, quite shortly, Hitchcock had been very disabused about his advocacy. With Gropius at Harvard and himself as something of a sponsor one might imagine his hopes, but the position to which, I think, he aspired now came to occupied by Sigfried Giedion.

A tragic or an amusing irony?

Anyway, the result became the publication of Giedion's *Space, Time and Architecture* (1941), an expanded version of the Charles Eliot Norton Lectures delivered in 1938–1939, which should deserve comparison with Hitchcock's *Modern Architecture: Romanticism and Reintegration* of twelve years earlier.

The two books cover the same historical terrain—from the later eighteenth century onward—but with *Space, Time and Architecture* Giedion achieved a major popular success which was denied the possibly more pioneering work of Hitchcock, so that, while the one became an architectural bible, the other remained largely an apocrypha. This is partly because the later date was more propitious—the English-speaking world was, at last, becoming interested in Modern architecture—and partly because Giedion placed his topic within an apparently more spacious intellectual milieu—within the highly pressured setting of an ultimately Hegelian worldview; and, perhaps most importantly, for the contribution of Herbert Bayer, himself a Bauhaus product, who was responsible for typography and layout. And this typography and layout do compel a recognition of Herbert Bayer's genius. For the look of the two books could not be more unlike. In 1929, Hitchcock's publishers presented his text up front and his visuals way, way back—way back even after the bibliographical note and index. But, in 1941, Herbert Bayer brought both text and visuals into the closest collaboration. Visuals are interspersed with text, and their captions even provide a textual alternative. A very great triumph! A mellifluous presentation which could only render Hitchcock's performance of 1929 slightly more dessicated?

Nevertheless, I felt way back and I still feel today that Hitchcock's is the superior judgement; and it is for this reason that I came to Yale, as they used to say, to sit at his feet. Rudy Wittkower had advised Harvard and Giedion; but, since I felt that this was a *something* about which he knew *nothing* (probably a pan-Germanic preference), I made my choice. And needless to say, at

Henry-Russell Hitchcock

Yale, I was never to hear anything good about either Walter Gropius or Sigfried Giedion.

Needless to say Hitchcock's lectures at Yale were, mostly, outstanding (he could switch from New York to Paris/London, from Chicago to Brussels/Glasgow/Amsterdam, with the greatest of ease; careers of clients were known in intimate detail); though to whom these lectures were supposed to be addressed I never quite understood. Likewise, for all his enthusiasm for Frank Lloyd Wright I could not quite understand his excitement; and, instead, I continued (and still continue) to endorse his remarks about Wright made in 1929:

> It is pertinent to remark here that his house interiors were never worthy of his exteriors despite the extraordinary thoroughness with which he studied their design and the excellence of his plans. His rooms were dark, uncomfortable and generally at once cluttered and monotonous. His efforts to make them light and playful only increased their self-conscious fussiness and self-righteous stodginess. Beside them Richardson's appear those of a master decorator.[4]

But I made an effort to conquer an aversion; and, after a year in New Haven, at Russell's instigation I began an extended tour of the United States, Canada, and Mexico, seeing something like forty Wright houses on the way—my preferred house being the Hardy House in Racine, Wisconsin.

It was a protracted tour—almost two years; and though I sometimes acted as a Limey scrounger, sometimes worked in offices in Vancouver and in Bakersfield, California, when I returned from Mexico very strapped for money, after a few weeks in Houston with fellow Yalie Howard Barnstone, I was greatly relieved—and even excited—to meet, in Norman, Oklahoma, Mrs. Harwell Hamilton Harris.

Notes

1. Bernard Berenson, *Sunset and Twilight* (New York: Harcourt Brace, 1963), 344.

2. The Berenson-Hitchcock *rencontre* was as Nicky Mariano's house up at Vallombrosa. It did not take place lower down at Settignano.

3. Colin Rowe, introduction to *Five Architects* (New York: Wittenborn, 1972), 4.

4. For H.R.H. on F.L.W. in 1929, see Henry-Russell Hitchcock, *Modern Architecture: Romanticism and Reintegration* (rpt. New York: Hacker Art Books, 1970), 115. For further Hitchcockian observations see my incomplete review of *Architecture: Nineteenth and Twentieth Centuries,* which is to be found later in this volume.

Henry-Russell Hitchcock

Texas and Mrs. Harris

Written 1988

It will be best to introduce the topic of Texas during the years 1953–1956 via the agency of a conversation I had with John Entenza in Chicago shortly before he died. We were having luncheon at the Drake Hotel and John was reminiscing about some of the extraordinary women who had been around in Los Angeles in the 1940s—Vera Stravinsky and Alma Mahler Gropius Werfel; then he said, "There was also Jean Murray Bangs, Mrs. Harwell Hamilton Harris, but, of course, Colin, you know something about her."

I suggested that he, probably, knew more, and, since he was delighted to continue, he told me that in 1920 or thereabouts, with two other women, the future Mrs. H. had walked all the way from Pasadena to Greenwich Village. "An early feminist no doubt," he said.

Myself first met Jean Harris in mid-April 1953 in Norman, Oklahoma, and this was a curious, meteorological experience

in itself. The skies were apocalyptic, threatening, almost purple—
like something that I have never elsewhere seen. It was a setting for
"The Fall of the House of Usher"; the immediate background was
Bruce Goff's school of architecture; also present was a distinctly intense Peruvian girl who lived in a primitive hut entirely lined with
black llama fur—floor, walls, *and* ceiling. Almost it was the final
chapter of Franz Kafka's *Amerika*—the nature theater of Oklahoma.
However, Mrs. H. dominated all this. She looked a little bit like the
Empress Catherine and abruptly she invited my presence in Austin
and so, inevitably, I obeyed. It was going to be either an Anglophile
or an Anglophobe occasion. But, after all, it was the equivalent of a
royal command, and it was thus that there was initiated my association with the University of Texas, where I joined the faculty in January of 1954.

   I spent the intervening time in New York, London, and
Paris. I came back to the U.S. on a beautiful, sumptuous old Cu-
narder of 1919, the *Samaria*. It had Grinling Gibbons and Robert
Adam saloons (equipped—believe it or not—with coal fires). To
the accompaniment of brilliant light, snow, and intense cold, this
entirely ravishing boat docked at Halifax, Nova Scotia, on January 1; and it was from the *Samaria* that I landed in New York on
January 2.

   I must have arrived in Austin about January 10, and, needless to say, I traveled in equally antique style. A night train from
Penn Station; a waking up around Terre Haute, Indiana; a change of
trains at St. Louis; another night train; a waking up somewhere in
Texas (Denison?); the disappearance of the last traces of snow at
Waxahachie; and then, increasingly, the traces of a new landscape—
live oaks, mesquite, tumbleweed, and, above all, with blue, blue
sky, something like the extreme blue of a Roman light in September. These were the prefaces to my arrival; and, of course, waiting at
the station there was Mrs. Harris.

   In one of her more tempestuous moods and with no notice
of my exhaustion, immediately she drove me off into that country
west of Austin (*barrancas,* incipient mesa formations, and more

tumbleweed), that country which can sometimes seem to be a minor version of Provence. We drove, I remember, through Lampasas; we drove through Llano; and always, on that brilliant January day, she talked and talked.

Her subject was academic politics and her object was to set me straight. There were two parties, pro- and anti-Harwell. It was the Empress Catherine all over again. Or, alternatively, it was Mme de Staël at Coppet. There were abominations, and then there was the possibility of a palace guard—in which I was to be an officer.

Supreme abominations were professors Buffler, McMath, and Roessner; and the palace guard, apart from me, was to comprise Hugo Leipziger-Pierce, Martin Kermacy, and Bernhard Hoesli. Also, among supreme abominations, were Marcus and Jean Whiffen.

Now to explain the role into which the excessively English Whiffens were cast will require a digression into Mrs. H.'s biography and psychology of which, only later, I became aware. She was born in British Columbia—Vancouver or Victoria; her mother migrated to Pasadena where Jean Murray Bangs must have matured well before 1914; and, as a result of this background, she always maintained a double allegiance. The most English of Canadians, she was also Californian, from the 'imperial' days of Teddy Roosevelt and William Howard Taft. But more than this she was Pasadena—long white gloves, lace fringes, visiting cards, all the apparatus of Pasadena of the great days. Then there had ensued that slightly wacky deviation, that hike across the country (alleged by John Entenza), with a subsequent, presumably Bohemian episode in New York. These were the antipodes of Mrs H.'s experience. *Femme forte et formidable,* her act was never harmonious. Greenwich Village of the twenties was always interactive with Edwardian Pasadena, and it was in terms of Pasadena that Mrs. Harris had rejected Mrs. Whiffen. Being English, Mrs. Whiffen ought to know better. Mrs. Whiffen was a masseuse, and how scandalous it was that the wife of a professor at the University of Texas should be so involved.

Texas and Mrs. Harris

By the time of my arrival in Texas this had become something of a cause célèbre. There had been a confrontation in the street, witnessed by Neil Lacey. Mrs. Scarborough (of the department store and The English Speaking Union) had taken the side of the Whiffens; and the next day (the day after my arrival) the Whiffens told me, "We have had the Czarina put under house arrest"; and this seemed to mean that the president of the University of Texas had forbidden Mrs. H. the campus. So I was amused that Marcus Whiffen had already cast Jean Harris in the role of Empress Catherine; and such was my first exposure to the academic politics of Texas.

Mrs. Harris, it must now be said, had been responsible for her husband's migration from Los Angeles to Austin. She had wished for him an equivalent to the academic position which Bill Wurster, as dean, had obtained at Berkeley; and she was prone to think of Catherine Bauer Wurster as a diabolical engineer of reputations. For had she not shifted Bill from Berkeley to MIT, and then—with increased status—back to Berkeley again? And had not these machinations placed Harwell in a scarcely to be tolerated predicament? For, intrinsically, was not Harwell the Prince of Wales awaiting installation on the imaginary throne of California architecture? And had not Mrs. Wurster usurped this manifest destiny? And, indeed, about the Harrises there was always something of the flavor of a court in exile. The rival school of redwood building had triumphed; but Jean Harris was now to redeem this usurpation in Texas where, very quickly, time was to discover truth.

Rather desperate it all seems; and rather desperate it certainly was. The Harrises lived in an indifferent house, with more than indifferent furniture. They had no pictures and few books; and, as I see it from the perspective of today, the reality of the story was late New Deal, like Eleanor Roosevelt camping out in one of those dreadful backgrounds—dull green walls, driftwood, chenille bedspreads—which displayed (and I wonder why) not a trace of evidence of her New York origins. In terms of rooms, the taste of Mrs. Harris, like that of Mrs. Roosevelt, was 'democratically' mute.

But Mrs. Harris, a genuinely great personage, could never, not even for a moment, allow herself to consider the acceptance of such a reputation as Mrs. Roosevelt's. Frenziedly isolationist, the staunchest of Republicans, she was able to find no excuse for the entry of the United States into either world war. She had never traveled. She had a reserved regard for England, but the mere idea of continental Europe provoked an excessive distaste. Though born in Canada she was, almost but not quite, *anima naturaliter Americana.*

At the time of my acquaintance with her I believe that she was writing articles on wine and food for *House Beautiful;* and she was certainly advising its editor, Elizabeth Gordon, on architectural matters. She was also allegedly writing a book on Greene and Greene—though persons like Russell Hitchcock took a somewhat different view. Hitchcock said that she was obstinately sitting on the Greene and Greene material. But this is more or less irrelevant to these recollections, and here it should be enough to note that the advice which Mrs. H. was transmitting to *House Beautiful* was of a distinctly embarrassing kind. The so-called International Style was an assault upon American values; the cult of Mies van der Rohe, very prevalent down in Houston, was part of the same insidious plot; and, therefore, it should not be surprising that about this time *House Beautiful* published an article with a prominent caption reading: "They are taking away your birthright for *this.*"

"This," of course, was the Farnsworth House; and, no less obviously, the birthright just had to be an item of California derivation—perhaps something like the Havens House in Berkeley by Harwell Harris himself. Such journalistic polemic must now be put into context. At this period there was exhibited the full mania and persecution of Joseph McCarthy's investigations; and if Jean Harris (in a maternal way, she was in love with my candid blue eyes) really wanted, in her wilder moments, to grab the junior senator from Wisconsin to join in an architectural crusade (a most unlikely possibility!), then a degree of circumspection might be enjoined.

However, in the conditions of that highly political city, Austin (I have always thought of it as a version of Stendhal's

Texas and Mrs. Harris

Parma), caution was scarcely possible; and there was no way in which I could escape the role of adviser.

Immediately upon my arrival, Mrs. H., the Czarina (she was also Bernini's Costanza Bonarelli), had made it evident that she would not permit any passive presence on my part; and then, the grand vizier of the Harris court, Hugo Leipziger, had also indicated my function: "Now [that] you have Colin you have a party." As a result, throughout February '54 there followed a series of meetings at the Harris house.

At these it was Mrs. Harris who, for the most part, presided; and Harwell was, for the most part, little more than a recessive note taker. Nor were Leipziger and Kermacy (older members of the 'palace guard') exactly forthcoming, and, soon, they ceased to attend. In other words, by late February our meetings were effectively comprised of Jean Harris, Bernhard Hoesli, and myself; and it was about this time that I first became aware of the Czarina's violent (violently possessive?) attitude toward her husband.

Harwell was taking notes, as seemed to be his big preoccupation; and, suddenly, to him his wife said: "Harwell, look at your silly, insipid, little handwriting! Just why don't you write big, like Bernhard?" An outburst so astonishing one is compelled to remember with accuracy, and this outburst was the first among many. But at this stage, I only wish to establish the motif. Because, for the present, it is Bernhard Hoesli who must command attention.

Swiss, from the canton of Glarus, a graduate of the Eidgenössische Technische Hochschule, perhaps three years younger than myself, Bernhard went on from Zurich to work for Le Corbusier in Paris; and, in Corbu's *Oeuvre Complète, 1946–52,* there is a picture of him, sort of *en profil perdu.* The occasion is Picasso's visit to the Unité at Marseilles; and, while down among the *pilotis* Picasso stands, stumpy and impassive, at center stage; and to the right (looking rather like an angel from some quattrocento Annunciation) Corbu gesticulates, in the left foreground and looking toward the masters, one will discover Bernhard; and, perhaps significantly, he is the only person in the group to be wearing a jacket.

Bernhard must have left the office in the rue de Sèvres shortly after this; and then, after a year in New York (?), he came to Texas at the same time as Harwell Harris, though not appointed by Harris.

Bernhard and I shared an office together for the five semesters that I was at the University of Texas; and, after 1961, I began to see him fairly frequently in Zurich. In fact, he became prime cause among several for visiting Zurich; but, all the same, when I first met him I was astonished by the person I found. To me, Bernhard seemed to be desperately anxious to shed the Corbusian influences which he had been privileged to acquire at first hand. The redeeming message now could only come from Spring Green, Wisconsin, and Scottsdale, Arizona; and, failing access to the source, it could only derive from such a Wrightian disciple as Harris. And the results of this about-face were a series of drawings which I still recollect. In effect, they were designs for dinky little ranchburgers, with a miserable entourage of hollyhocks, delphiniums, etc. More or less the lower-middle-class Wright of the Depression years.

In other words, my first exposures to Bernhard were not entirely gratifying. I had just completed a tour in which I had seen an awful lot of Wright houses; and, for me, this experience had dissipated the mystique. Mostly I had found them gruesome/lugubrious/coercive, and I suppose that I must have made this evaluation highly evident and remonstrated with Bernhard for what I, probably, called his apostasy.

Anyway, my relation with Bernhard certainly began something like this, and, almost certainly, the style and the substance of our meetings with the Harrises were slanted to F.L.W. It was evident that there was no hope of proposing anything whatsoever unless it involved a conspicuous Wrightian component. So, with this conceded, I then moved off into casuistry. I proposed that Theo van Doesburg was not so much affiliated with Analytical Cubism as he was an abstraction of Wright, and I further proposed that the Maison Domino of Le C. was, itself, no more than an abstraction of the structure of all those Chicago buildings in the Loop.

Texas and Mrs. Harris

These conclusions, plausible but slightly specious, were embodied in a memorandum which Hoesli and I sent to Harris at the
beginning of March 1954, a memorandum which seems to elude rediscovery and about which I shall have more to say. But, meanwhile, it was the substance of this message, intimating a triangle
of relevant achievement comprised of the productions of Wright,
Mies, and Corbu, which quickly led to significant hirings, with
Hoesli proposing the name of John Hejduk, whom he had met in
New York and who had then gone on to a Fulbright scholarship in
Rome, and with myself, because of my experience at Yale, suggesting an input from the studio of Josef Albers. This because the
rigor and the elegance of the Albers studio appeared to me to be
completely exemplary. Albers was just the best thing going; and, in
proposing graduates of the Albers studio, I quickly was able to discover that Harwell Harris also had an enthusiasm for it. He had
been a visiting critic at Yale and, for him too, it was quite the best.

So the new teachers arrived in September '54. Apart from
Hejduk, from Yale there were Robert Slutzky, Lee Hirsche, and Irwin Rubin, and these three rapidly encouraged the Texas students
to draw like angels. The drawings the students made, under an Albers dispensation, were of an economy which was outstanding; and today I would say that it was from these arrivals that there began the
great brilliance of a very brief Texas performance. A performance in
which the students were excessively stimulated and in which, I suspect, they particularly responded to the passionately cool teachings
of Slutzky. However, all was not well.

The results of this new teaching were to promote Le Corbusier and Mies, but not F.L.W.; and this *soon* became obvious. In
spite of my politics the Czarina fumed: we were being disloyal to
America. And what about these un-American names—Hejduk,
Slutzky, Hirsche—but *these* just *wouldn't* do. And, in this strange,
racist obsession, both Bernhard and I thought that Jean Harris—
Jean Murray Bangs, Costanza Bonarelli, the Empress Catherine—
was operating under the conniving influence of Hugo Leipziger.
We might very well have been wrong but such is what we believed,

and the ultimate denouement of all this passion and infatuation occurred in November '54.

Harwell was absent from town on one of those field trips, which were always his primary interest; he had taken a group of students to visit the Calcasieu Lumber Company. Was this in Nacogdoches or Natchitoches? Was it in east Texas or Louisiana? However, no matter. The absence of Harwell had provided the pretext for a confrontation. I was summoned by the Czarina to appear for something like tea; and, as I now see it, this occasion was the beginning of the end of our little pedagogical experiment, after scarcely more than two months' trial.

Mrs. H. lay on the floor and frequently drummed her heels upon it. I believe that she thought that she was, shortly, to die of cancer, and the scene was pure Dostoevski. There was no tea to drink; and she just ranted.

> Tell me about Hoesli, tell me what he's been doin'! Did he take that woman to Colorado last year? Did he take her to Mexico this year? Doesn't he know that it's a federal offense to take a girl across a state line for improper purposes? Doesn't he know that's why Wright got into trouble— takin' a girl across a state line for improper purposes? Doesn't he know that Buffler and McMath, if they get to hear this, will use it against Harwell? You've got to tell Hoesli that he has either to give her up, marry her at once, or resign his position. And if you can't or won't do that then you will be disloyal to Harwell.

All of this repeated and repeated.

It seems incredible but, all the same, this is not a scene which I have the capacity to invent, and her words were so extraordinary that I have found them unforgettable. The 'woman' or 'girl' concerned was Margaret Schostag from Corpus Christi, a secretary. I believe she was in a lawyer's office down by the State Capitol, and I suppose that the information about her must have been con-

Texas and Mrs. Harris

veyed by Hugo Leipziger and, certainly, this is what Bernhard also supposed. Because while I told Mrs. H. that under no circumstances would I divulge the substance of her hysterical *démarche* to Hoesli, of course I did so and, some months later, Bernhard did marry Margaret Schostag. They were married by the Bishop and I was best man, but I remain entirely unconvinced that Mrs H.'s dictations had anything to do with this 'solution.'

So Bernhard and Margaret went on to live in a charming little house where everything was white and where (overtones of Adolf Loos) the curtains were white chintz. However, this virginal setting for a *jeune ménage* was established somewhat later, and the immediate upshot of my afternoon with Jean Harris was that the situation was now irretrievably rifted. There was the primary rift between the Harrises and most of the older faculty and now this secondary rift between Mrs. Harris and, as it turned out, all of the younger faculty. After that afternoon, in November '54, not any of our immediate colleagues wished to have anything more to do with Mrs. H.

But now to approach the affair of the summer school of '55. It had become a prerogative of the older faculty to teach the summer school; but since we younger faculty were paid a very meager salary, we were of the opinion that employment in the summer school, apart from securing a continuity of our teaching, would be a very useful help; and we lobbied accordingly.

So attention must now be shifted to the final faculty meeting of the year—late April '55. It opened with Harris reading a letter from the president of the university apropos of Buffler, McMath, and Roessner. It appeared that these gentleman needed to teach the summer school (I think that these were the exact words); and, as a result, that they *must* be appointed—that is alongside Hoesli, Hejduk, and myself.

This, of course, was an unbearable affront to Harris, and he sat without speaking while the younger group, perhaps too explosively, rallied to his defense. Then, but only after the younger faculty had thoroughly exposed itself, he twisted his hands (this was a characteristic gesture—he had rather large and Michelangelesque hands) and made his final announcement. He was resigning his position as chairman and he was going to open an office in Fort Worth.

It must be obvious that, from then onward, the younger faculty were like so many lambs awaiting slaughter; and the first massacre very quickly occurred. Hejduk, Slutzky, Hirsche, Rubin, and myself very shortly received letters telling us that after the spring semester of '56, our appointments would not be renewed. Though I was separately informed that, since I was a "scholar and a gentleman" (shades of the deep, deep South), so long as I simply taught history and theory, my own position was assured.

The rest of the story is very simple. In the summer of '56, all of us, with the exception of Hoesli, left—myself in a fit of trade-union solidarity, and, while Hejduk and Slutzky had been of the opinion that Hoesli should have left along with me, Bernhard remained, and he acted to inculcate a new faculty arriving in the fall.

These were Lee Hodgden, Werner Seligmann, and John Shaw, and it is thus possible at this period to speak of a second 'school of Texas' linked to the first only through the personality of Bernhard Hoesli.

However, the second 'school of Texas' proved to be no more permanent than the first; and, after not many months, in the early summer of '57, its members received notice that their contracts would, also, not be renewed after the summer of '58. But this time the dismissals included Bernhard; and it was thus there followed a diaspora.

Bernhard returned to Zurich and the E.T.H. Werner Seligmann left for Germany and afterward joined Hoesli in Switzerland; Lee Hodgden led an exodus of Texas students to Oregon; and John Shaw went to do graduate work at MIT, later to spend three years in North Carolina.

Not by chance, I believe, but by the agency of Werner Seligmann (a Cornell graduate of the period of Richard Meier and Peter Eisenman), this little group—with the obvious exception of Bernhard—reassembled itself at Cornell in the years '61–'62. Werner and Lee came to Ithaca in '61 and John came in '62. It all be-

Texas and Mrs. Harris

came a bit like a celebration of Texas a few years back, had it not
been for the presence of myself. Because somehow my own prove-
nance didn't quite fit.

Myself spent the year '57–'58 as visiting critic at Cornell;
and then, allured by a flattering invitation I went on to spend four
years at the University of Cambridge. Mildly rewarding but also
highly frustrating these years happened to be. The presence of
King's College Chapel, "that glorious work of fine intelligence," was
never quite enough; and therefore, when ultimately dismayed by
the policies of Leslie Martin (incidentally, a version of Harwell Harris, 'liberals' both but 'intellectuals' neither), I returned to Cornell
in '62. At this stage I began to perceive a problem.

Somehow, with Lee, John, and Werner I was not entirely
authentic. I came from Texas—of course I did—but I belonged to
an earlier dispensation. Earlier by two and a half years. The great
revelation had been vouchsafed to Bernhard; and, as for me, I was
apocryphal, very little more than an Old Testament curiosity.

But *what* a sweat and, personal paranoia apart, my predicament must have been observed by students. Hence the term *the
Texas Rangers:*

> Oh I am a Ranger and I come from Texas
> Oh I am a Ranger and I'm teaching you
> We are Lee, John, and Werner and we are all Rangers
> Just git you an outfit and you'll be one too.

This was obviously to the tune of "The Streets of Laredo,"
and it possessed an alternative final line which referred to the *Oeuvre
Complète* of Le Corbusier: "Just git you the good book and you'll be
one too."

To repeat: at this time I had just come to teach at Cornell
for good (or, maybe, for bad); and as a consequence there was a still
further song:

Oh the Rangers come from Texas,
There's Werner, John, and Lee,
And Colin's come from Cambridge,
No Texas Ranger he.

But these songs are cited so as to establish that the term *the Texas Rangers* was first articulated at Cornell, in fifth-year studio language, during the fall of 1962; and, as I remember, it first erupted in the songs of either Alan Chimacoff or Tom Schumacher, who were then fifth-year students with an aptitude for writing songs ("J. S. Bach's Fifth Brandenburg Concerto has a harpsichord cadenza"—and ever so many more).

But should it not be obvious that the term the Texas Rangers belongs to the theater of New York Jewish irony and that it could scarcely have originated in Texas itself? It is a kindly, though sardonic, ex post facto designation applied, by Jewish wit, to three Cornell faculty members who were at the University of Texas in '56–'57.

All the more astonishing therefore that a questionnaire addressed to Harwell Harris in September '86 refers to "the hiring of 'the Texas Rangers' group" with which, of course, Harris had nothing whatsoever to do. And, still more astonishing that Harris, in responding to this questionnaire, should be able to use the same terminology. But, apparently, with the elapse of fewer than twenty-five years, Cornell studio language of 1962 had already become the provision of Texas myth.

P.S. I appreciate the fact that my account of Mrs. Harris will scarcely seem credible—to those who never met her. Hence I will cite an occasion when she made a completely public display of her temperament. There were about thirty people in the room, and Harwell was sitting on some sort of settee at one end—rather surprisingly with his hands behind his back. So Mrs. H. saw this from the other end of the room, and, with no thought of what anybody present might think, from about twenty feet away she called out: "Har-

Texas and Mrs. Harris

well, *what* are you doing with your hands? Put them out in front of you *immediately.*" Needless to say, Harwell did so.

But this sort of thing became almost commonplace, and it is thus that one should understand the president of the University of Texas forbidding her presence on the campus. (But could he have been in a position to do this? Or was this story, mostly, the Whiffens' gossip?) As I have already implied, Mrs. Harris was a distinguished, ambitious, and tragically frustrated woman, and I believe that she was particularly frustrated in her maternal instincts—thus her attitude toward her husband, thus her concern with Bernhard's sex life, thus her preoccupation with me. These frustrations must have promoted her characteristic style of hysterical overreaction.

On the other hand, by John Entenza I was given an alternative explanation: that at the time of her marriage to Harwell (and she was considerably older than he) she had rescued him from incipient alcoholic tendencies. But this might have been no more than the Los Angeles gossip of the day. Of course, neither explanation excludes the other; and, for a long time, I hadn't thought of either until beginning to write this memorandum.

When were the Harrises married? It would be interesting to know, for I suspect that by that time she was already beyond the menopause. So was their 'joining together' ever consummated? Or did it remain *mariage blanc?* I speculate and will never know. Likewise, whatever happened in Greenwich Village of the early twenties is now beyond rediscovery.

However, I don't suppose that the identification of Mrs. Harris with the Empress Catherine, made by the Whiffens, myself, and others, could have been entirely separated from a related pattern of sexual behavior. Of course, at no time can I think that she was the victim of insatiability; and I am merely suggesting that, in this psychological territory, there is to be discovered a further explanation of her bizarre conduct. I can only hypothesize that, frustrated in love (as I think she was) and frustrated by age, this California/Texas Czarina had turned for satisfaction to private fantasies of the most lurid politics. For, in the 1950s, for a woman of her passion, brilliance, and ambitions, what other outlet could she have than her husband's academic politics? (Not that he had any.)

Poor, poor woman, whom I still regard and lament and whom, after this great interval of time, I still envision in the sharpest focus! Intelligent and highly engaging as she was, it was the sequence of her generally calamitous action which obliged her husband's withdrawal from Texas and which rendered brief and ultimately impotent that somewhat naive pedagogical experiment initiated, under her auspices, by Bernhard Hoesli and myself.

P.P.S. Of the recent quasi-canonization of Harwell Harris by the University of Texas and his new status as legendary and martyred guru, I hear the talk but I cannot pretend to know the details.

However, see a letter from Carter Manny which Harris quotes as part of his response to David Thurman's questionnaire of September 1986 (toward the end of an invitation to Harris to speak at the Graham Foundation). Carter Manny writes: "And whatever you might have to tell us about 'the Texas Rangers' at Texas University [sic] would probably also influence the younger generation of architects in Chicago, who have been so influenced by them. So maybe you should fill me in on the Rangers so I will have something more to tell my Chicago audience." [1]

This is symptomatic of the vitality of the legend inadvertently propagated by Alan Chimacoff and Tom Schumacher. Without *their* songs, 'the Texas Rangers' would never have been heard of. But it must be insisted that these songs relate to a situation at Cornell in the early 1960s rather than to any situation existing in Texas a few years earlier. Without Chimacoff's and Schumacher's charming and juvenile interventions, Cornell pedagogic practice of the sixties and onward would never have been antedated (even authenticated?) by providing it with a certificate of origin in Texas.

But what does all this add up to? Not, as far as I can perceive, to any 'insemination' by Harwell Harris in Texas. Simple chronology excludes the Texas Rangers of the song from having any contact with Harris; the contacts between Hejduk and Harris were

Texas and Mrs. Harris

minimal, and within two months they were finished; while the allegiance of Slutzky, Hirsche, and Rubin was to Josef Albers.

So this restricts any Harris 'insemination' of the Texas faculty to Bernhard and to me; and, about this, what do I say of myself? Always impatient of blood and soil ideologies, never seduced by the mystique of 'native' California redwood, I was invited to Texas not by Harwell Harris but by the animation of his wife; and my loyalties, so long as they were able to exist, were to her. Simply, I found that Harwell had nothing significant to say and nothing, of any kind, to contribute; and this is why, for a couple of months, I served as his speechwriter.

Whether or not the archives of the U. of T. disclose this function of mine I do not know, but I am told that, in Zurich, the Hoesli archives at the E.T.H. do. This because dearest Bernhard, like any good Swiss, was a filing cabinet addict and would never allow any piece of paper to escape his possession; the *apologia pro vita sua* related to the documents.

This is to intimate that any influence of Harwell Harris on his faculty could only relate to his relationship with Hoesli; and, after my arrival and my Corbu/Mies propaganda, this relationship was, necessarily, diminished.

So, in order to understand (should you wish to) whatever happened at Texas during those years, you have to forget about Harwell and begin to think about Jean Harris—the Czarina and Bernini's Costanza Bonarelli—particularly in terms of Hoesli and myself. For, to repeat, the significant hirings of '54 came, entirely, as the result of our suggestions. Meanwhile, it pleases me to believe that, almost certainly, Bernhard would have agreed with most of this account which I have given.

Note

1. See letter by Harris of October 14, 1986, written in response to a questionnaire prepared by David Thurman in preparation for a thesis at the University of Texas, 1988.

Comments of Harwell Hamilton Harris to the Faculty, May 25, 1954

> *Will no one tell me what she sings?*
> *Perhaps the plaintive numbers flow*
> *For old, unhappy, far off things*
> *And battles long ago.*

If I, sometimes, think of the Texas of way back in terms of Wordsworth's "solitary highland lass . . . reaping and singing by herself," I hope that I have made it abundantly clear that there was nothing inscrutable about Mrs. Harris. Peremptory, predatory rather than plaintive, she never cajoled but always demanded. This was the Empress Catherine in her and, accordingly, both Bernhard Hoesli and myself became conscripted, with no possibility of escape, into her service.

Therefore, what here follows is an unpublished memorandum written at her insistence partly by Bernhard but mostly, I think, by myself. Writ-

ten in March of 1954, it was then delivered by Harwell in the following May—as his very own thoughts.

But how to distinguish Bernhard's contributions from my own at a time when both he and I wished to shift attention from personalities to principles and from politics to policies, at a time when neither of us had any philosophical dispute beyond the problems of English flippancy and Zurich seriosità?

But, of course, Bernhard did enjoy the precedence. Long before my own arrival he was firmly established as persona grata with Mr. and Mrs. H., and it was only later that the two of us became installed as a couple of Wunderkinder *and that, rather like advisers to a highly inept president, we became indispensable as a pair of speechwriters.*

In any case it was Bernhard who kept all of the documents—like what follows and so many others which I am not interested to recall; and, as contemporary 'history', most of these are preserved at the E.T.H. in Zurich.

All the same, reading this stuff after a very great lapse of time, I believe that I can still recall the activity of different pencils and typewriters. At bottom, as it now appears to me, both of us were highly ingenuous and highly ignorant Hegelians. Like Peter Eisenman and so many others at the present day, we were both consumed by the myth (?) of an all-controlling and perceptible Zeitgeist. *The spirit of the age was accessible. It possessed a coercive tangibility. But if the most deadly of deadly sins was to commit an anachronism, while Bernhard was concerned to present the nuts and the bolts, the nitty-gritty of the faith which we both shared, it was myself who was much more generalized and expansive.*

So there were Mrs. Harris and her husband, whose not very effectual voice may, occasionally, be detected in what follows; and, then, there was Bernhard, determined to articulate the specifics of a curriculum; and, then, there was me, who had largely excerpted passages from a review, written two years before, of Talbot Hamlin's Forms and Functions of Twentieth Century Architecture. *And just what did that Texas faculty think of this production?*

Since they were, mostly, incapable of assembling ideas, probably it is safe to say that this memorandum was received like water on the back of the proverbial duck. Just words, words, words (as though a verbal message

could be anything else); but, had that faculty possessed any traces of intellec-
tual agility, just how successfully could it have roasted this little memoran-
dum? But it was to take a long time to recognize that the aperçus *and the*
problems propounded by Hegel were not a revelation of eternal truth and that
Modern architecture was not a Kantian imperative.

However, separate from all this, addressed by the Wunderkinder
to the boss, there was that more private memorandum addressed, also, to those
of the faculty who were not rabidly anti-Harris; and, with reference to Mrs.
H., I have already referred to the critical opposition of two diagrams, the im-
plied dialectic between Le Corbusier's Maison Domino and almost any one of
those axonometric projections of Theo van Doesburg (fig. 3); and, of course,
this was a pretty simpleminded distinction.

It was based on Hitchcock's Painting toward Architecture
(New York, 1948); and its evident purpose was to open up a critical um-
brella for the importation of other than Wrightian models. Or, if you like, it
was to provide a critical visa, an all-American alibi for the admission of
Mies and Corbu. A too ingenuous, too simple expedient? But, in what ap-
peared to be a mishmash land, an intellectual desert, an unstructured void,
what else do you do but resort to simple expedience? You cook and you play
with the ingredients available; you try what you can do; you do not assume
metropolitan sophistication—if desirable that may come later. But this little
memo, for all of its insufficiency, had almost the effect of a demolition of the
Berlin Wall. It seemed to permit a flow of air. To me it still seems to have per-
mitted the appointments of John Hejduk (Farnese Hercules in propria persona) *and the representatives of Josef Albers. And the results were limpid*
purity.

Almost, then, "it was bliss in that dawn to be alive"; and, indeed,
we were quite ecstatic. After the more than corrupt renderings, the dissolute
Beaux-Arts horrors to which our eyes had not *become accustomed, with the*
new arrivals at Texas we had begun to comprise a very excited little society.
And not a day went by without its pleasures.

These meetings at the end of each year are intended to review the
work of the past year and to suggest ways in which the work ahead
may be improved. This seems a worthwhile purpose, and I was sur-

Comments of Harwell Harris to the Faculty

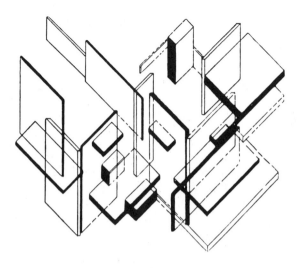

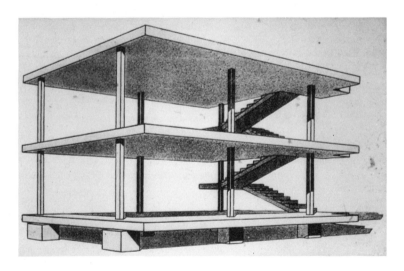

3. Theo van Doesburg, *Counter-Construction*, 1922; Le Corbusier, Maison Domino, 1922.

prised to discover in the two previous meetings of this kind that I attended that so little suggestion and agreement came of it.

A more recent meeting which we had, called for the purpose of formulating a list of objectives of the School asked for in the questionnaire of the Accrediting Board, likewise failed to accomplish anything at all. I was more surprised at this because I had expected that you who had a hand in the formation of the curriculum—both the present one and previous ones on which the present one was built—would surely have a number of objectives in mind and would express them strongly.

I recall these earlier meetings because their failure to initiate anything is responsible for my decision to assume the initiative in the present instance.

A clearly stated philosophy of architectural education is necessary if we are to have either a clear understanding of objectives or a basis for intelligent criticism of our teaching procedures. It is apparent that this is what we lack.

These meetings are not the only place in which this lack has been felt. The need for a philosophy has recently been pointed up by charges that a student has obtained his design by copying. This copying is not a simple matter of a student's morals. We cannot put the blame squarely on the student, as we would if he were found appropriating his neighbor's answers in a mathematics exam; for he is doing little more than what he sees others doing—some of them the largest and most emulated firms in the profession—taking a little here and a little there until an entire design is assembled.

The blame is really ours. Because we give him no principles of design, he is aware only of effects. We avoid the responsibility of installing any idea in the mind of the student by declaring that we don't want to influence him. In so doing we toss him to the magazines and all other dealers in the most recent effects. In leaving him to the magazines we are abdicating as teachers. We are critics in the narrowest sense of the term—accepting or rejecting, never informing. Originality is determined according to the copyright laws

Comments of Harwell Harris to the Faculty

protecting musicians: so many bars of continuous copy from a single source is reminiscence; any more is plagiarism. Thus is superficiality built in.

As a state institution we have obligations to the State of Texas. As a professional School we have obligations to the architects of Texas. Our still primary obligations are to our students. For the present we shall confine our discussion to our student obligations, which are two:

1. To equip the student with the skills necessary for the practice of his profession; and
2. To enable him to develop his powers of selection by the process of his own judgement.

By making possible on the part of the student a series of progressive judgements we are responsible in the course of five years for a significant modification of his personality. This is a serious responsibility, and therefore, before we promote judgements in others, we should concern ourselves with an examination of the values upon which our own judgements are based.

An academy—and a school of architecture is an academy—is by its nature obliged to be academic. It is in consequence committed to a belief in knowledge and a respect for theories of education. It assumes cultural self-consciousness to be a virtue. It can exist only by reference to a body of ideas. Its educational program cannot be founded upon irresponsible opinion, private preference, or individual fantasy, but must be rooted in the understanding and respect for certain general principles. These general principles can form a frame of reference within which legitimate differences of opinion among faculty can exist. It is necessary to consider what frame of reference we can legitimately assume to be our own.

The student's discovery of intellectual clarity, reason, and order must be made within the specific structure of the present time. Otherwise he is unable to act. His act—his creation, his self-expression—is irrelevant unless related to (1) the technical equipment and (2) the educated artistic will of the present day. He must be led, step by step, to an appreciation of these.

It cannot be assumed that the present day is without an overt artistic urge, will, volition. No earlier time has been without one and there is no reason to believe that we are exempted from what has so far been universal. That modern architecture is not merely a negative rationalism, that it embodies a positive will, is proved by evidences which are daily before our eyes. It therefore becomes our duty to reveal these evidences to the student.

The suspension of judgement upon the present day, of which all are at some time guilty, is usually explained as a respect for the student's freedom of choice. But, instead of respect, it is in fact irresponsibility. Freedom of choice cannot exist without information, and information can hardly be considered bias. Only from a background of knowledge can the student be expected to make a free, emancipated choice.

To emphasize the present is not to repudiate the past. Only through the present can we understand the past. By discovering the will of his own time the student is able to understand the wills of other times. In assessing the present he is making an historical judgement. In seeing the present as the most recent historical sequence, he is able to escape the present. By recognizing that certain creative acts are possible only at a certain moment in history, one is able to think of the future as something other than a perpetuation of the present. Attachment to the present prevents an anachronistic lapse into the past, and an understanding of the past prevents a belief in the present as a final and definite state. It is this historical judgement of the present and this contemporary judgement of history which alone can sanction a critical standard to which all can give assent.

A present-day vocabulary has developed so far that the teacher cannot expect his students to do other than work within it. It is their choice, not his. In addition to the vocabulary there are the systems of order expressed with it. It is not the teacher's job to prefer the abstract order or the organic order, but to help the student

Comments of Harwell Harris to the Faculty

to investigate and analyze the different systems of logic so that he can tell the difference between the central tradition of modern architecture and the imitations of it. The student who cannot distinguish the real from the imitation remains preoccupied with the threadbare stereotypes of commercial art.

Acceptance of the existence of a formal vocabulary may be objected to as an endorsement of copying and a license of the hero worship of particular architects. But has a creative act ever been performed in a vacuum?

Originality may often express itself suddenly but never without some previous experience with form. Without such experience the student in his attempt to be original will generally end by being arbitrary.

Imitation is a method of assimilation. In accepting it as such the student gains knowledge and experience and is the quicker thereby to discover his own originality.

In turning from a survey of standards to one of techniques, it will be observed that the confusion of values becomes apparent here in a confusion of systems.

Two major systems have within the past fifty years enjoyed a conspicuous success—those of the Ecole des Beaux-Arts and of the Bauhaus. This simple statement is by no means to commend the results of either but merely to observe that both have possessed to a high degree a generating power, and that both have to some extent been able to endow their techniques with universal significance. Neither in the light of the present day appears completely adequate for our requirements.

According to present critical patterns, the first influence is now condemned and the second is identified with enlightenment and progress. In the general understanding the first is associated with a derivative classicism and the second with the authentic tradition of modern architecture. Such an interpretation should not impede an analysis of their respective merits.

The doctrine of the Ecole des Beaux-Arts revolved around the organization of architectural material according to the principles of composition and the infusing of that material with a symbolic content usually referred to as character. According to the theory, neither correct composition nor appropriate character was sufficient in itself. Both must be present, and the existence of the one was not automatically productive of the other. Guadet spoke of character as the identity between the architectural and moral impressions of the problem, but like other theorists of the period he recognized that the demand for character was a fairly recent innovation, and that neither Antiquity nor the Middle Ages had made of character a matter of capital importance.

Neither composition nor character were among the acknowledged or conscious preoccupations of the Bauhaus, which envisaged architecture as an interaction of function and techniques and which, seeing form as their automatic consequence, distrusted problems of composition insofar as they are problems of form. Similarly, since the Bauhaus was disposed in its productions to exemplify the typical, it showed an equal distrust for problems of character.

Thus by what will to some appear as a distortion of the problem, the Bauhaus was able to achieve significant results, but it is also possible that during the last fifty years the demand for the *characteristic* has indeed diminished and that a preference for the *typical* now enjoys a certain force. This is to commend neither one nor the other but merely to bring the matter to serious attention, to indicate that the antithesis *type* versus *character* does not exist and that neither can be set up as an exclusive criterion. Moreover it is evident that visual appearance is the *result* of character and that therefore character itself cannot be achieved by a mere manipulation of visual effects. Character must obviously be an *implicit* quality before it can become an *explicit* quality.

But from the standpoint of the present day it can be seen how, in conscious opposition to the accepted tenets of academic eclecticism and as a matter of polemical efficiency, the Bauhaus did indeed oversimplify the problems of architecture. In the mental climate of the 1920s this point of view was both necessary and under-

Comments of Harwell Harris to the Faculty

standable, and its success can be judged by the state of creative
impotence to which it has reduced all older pedagogic disciplines.
It now seems clear that the Bauhaus, in its professed disregard for
problems of form, denied the artistic volition which was the motivation of its own experiment. It was disposed to see the *technical* rather
than the *cultural* milieu of the 1920s as unique, and thus, in disre-
garding certain aspects of the contemporary, it came to disregard
the past and to see the future merely as a perpetuation of the present. Primarily it was a reaction against, and as soon as the academi-
cism it had attacked had lost vigor, so also its springboard had
disappeared.

In a more subtle way the Beaux-Arts showed an equal disregard for history, which it was apt to see as no more than a reservoir of possible compositional motifs. Implying the process and
problems of composition to have been at all times identical with its
own, it made of history a common denominator rather than a pro-
gression. Although it did not, like the Bauhaus, declare artistic volition to be an irrelevance, it promoted the idea that in all ages it had
been the same. Thus the Beaux-Arts, like the Bauhaus, was indisposed to recognize the unique circumstances of either its own or any
other historical moment, and came to see the *past* merely as a perpetuation of the present.

These merely partial realizations of the contemporary are
wholly inadequate for our purpose, and their ensuing idolatries of
past and future are both apt to vitiate the possibilities of significant
achievement in the present. In the one case it becomes impossible,
and in the other it can be indefinitely postponed. Thus it is proposed neither to revive the Beaux-Arts nor to erect a new Bauhaus,
but merely to indicate that since in the recent past both have affected us, neither can be overlooked, and that from the remnants
of both it is possible that by a process of trial and error something
of significance might be constructed.

It was inevitable perhaps that at the moment of its success
Gropius's very distinct core of doctrine should also become practi-
cally invalidated. In the larger context its results were destructive.

TEXAS, PRE-TEXAS, CAMBRIDGE

In the matter of the plan this situation has had disastrous results only too evident on examination of student designs in schools throughout the country. The conception that any rationale of planning exists is apparently no longer entertained. That specific consequences belong to specific shapes seems only rarely to be understood, so that planning, rather than a matter of spatial logic, has come to be no more than a matter of functional expediency.

It is not accidental that, of the two contemporary architects for whom the plan appears of the most explicit importance, both should have received influences from the Beaux-Arts, and a revaluation of its contribution to planning would seem to be apt. Aberrant and grandiose as most of its exercises seem to present-day taste, there is no doubt that this French approach exhibited towards planning a richness of information, an analytical power, an inventiveness of parti, and a disciplined capacity for rapid judgement. Seeing the planning process as a sort of primary mental gymnastic, the generator of architectural form, it was at its best able to arrive at highly succinct, unambiguous conclusions. It is precisely these aptitudes which require a renewed emphasis at the present day, and which we should make every effort to reestablish.

Transferring our attention from the general to the specific, it is observed that the student reaches the peak of his enthusiasm in the Sophomore and Junior years. From then it declines until, in the Fifth year, he is ready for almost any compromise in order to get out of school. His natural receptiveness is either mutilated or buried. It will take him years to reestablish it as one of his most valuable gifts.

Explanations for this state of affairs have already been suggested in the present condition of critical standards, which leads to a consideration of only the mechanical aspects of contemporary order, resulting in a confusion of educational objectives and an ensuing incapacity for selection. Added to this may be cited the overemphasis on originality, which requires performance on a basis merely of technical knowledge. We have, in fact, reached a condition in which the process of instruction is regarded too exclusively

Comments of Harwell Harris to the Faculty

as one of mining—an extraction of material from the student and a giving of very little back. To remedy this situation we may conclude that certain actions on our part are immediately possible:

It is proposed that a lecture course equivalent to that formerly known as theory of architecture be inaugurated, consisting of one hour of formal lecture per week in each semester, beginning with the Sophomore year. This course would concern itself with structural media and the rationale of planning. Within it historical and contemporary examples would be exhibited, but each would be assessed within the framework of its own terminology, and it would always be made clear that each represents the solution of an architectural problem in a cultural situation which, like that of the present day, is unique and wholly distinct.

It is proposed that these discussions include organic as well as inorganic order. In the study of natural form there will be discovered, in infinite variety, examples of internal order, development from within outward, continuity of idea, continuity of structure, interdependence of parts, integrity, simplicity, homogeneity, and sequence. The example of nature provides the discipline of a great ideal, one that yields rich rewards to the architect in search of principle. Forms and materials are seen to have individual natures, and behavior according to individual nature is seen to constitute virtue, integrity, beauty. Organic order is the prime example of the coordinating effect of the operation of principle.

It is also proposed that the courses in drawing be recast as a means of apprehending form as well as representing it. One only sees fully when he expresses what he sees. The expression is primarily for himself. It is the equivalent to words in the formation of his thoughts. It makes his thoughts precise. It preserves them, enabling him to reexamine and reflect upon them, to trace patterns and discover relationships. It makes possible more lengthy and more complex calculations than are possible when all figures must be carried in one's head. The separation between freehand drawing and mechanical drawing is largely arbitrary and needs to be seen as not so much a means of presenting reality as a method of abstracting it.

TEXAS, PRE-TEXAS, CAMBRIDGE

Drawing and perspective must involve the discovery of the nature and the structure of objects and not merely the facts of their accidental appearance.

It is proposed that there be established a coordination of the work of the student in his drawing and his design courses. This coordination will follow throughout all but the Freshman year.

It is proposed that there be an enlargement of the scope of the critic's work to include formal lectures in the theory of architecture as already described, and occasional projects of a collaborative nature in which the critic becomes leader. It is proposed that there be an enlargement of the scope of the jury's work to include previews at preliminary stages in the project's development, and reviews at the project's conclusion.

As implements of the design program it is planned to provide two manuals. One manual is for teachers and will outline for the guidance of the Design Faculty the policy and methods of the School. The other manual is for students and will provide a similar service for them.

The work on these manuals is already under way. Some of you have already made contributions to them, and others of you will be asked to assist.

Lockhart, Texas

Written 1955–1956; published in *Architectural Record*, 1957

*I was first taken to Lockhart by Mrs. Harris, and therefore she is ulti-
mately responsible for this article. I paid a second visit to Lockhart
with John Hejduk, who was as excited as I originally was, and so we
paid another visit in which John took the pics and I did the scribbling.
This article was intended as a contribution to a possible series about
small-town America which I have not been able to pursue. Perhaps the
U.S. is too big to know anything in detail, as one is able to know
things in Italy. But I would have liked to have written about the
American small town as I have seen it in many other locations—in
Texas, Llano and Lampasas; in Alabama, Demopolis and Selma;
in Michigan, Jackson and Marshall; in New York, Cazenovia and
Skaneateles.*

Somewhere or other Gertrude Stein says that certainly America is
the oldest country in the world, and if it may be supposed that she

was simply straining a paradox, there is a perceptiveness in her re-
mark which travelers in the United States sooner or later come to
recognize, although the observation itself is perhaps one which
could only have been made by an American expatriate returning
to the American West. Certainly it is there, where the strata of historical activity are so few and where time has contrived to erode so
little of the little past that exists, that there will sometimes be experienced a feeling of inextinguishable antiquity.

This is a quality which evades any immediate definition;
but often in the sharp light and the vacant landscape of the West architectural detail will seem to achieve an almost archaic clarity, so
that the most tawdry saloon or incrusted false facade may acquire a
portentous distinction, while whole towns founded no earlier than
the sixties can exude an Italian evidence of age. For these reasons,
for the sympathetic traveler Utah will evoke memories of Tuscany;
Virginia City, Nevada, will appear a nineteenth-century Urbino;
while such mining cities as Leadville, Colorado, Carson City, Nevada, or Globe, Arizona, will seem as unquestionably as Gubbio or
Siena to have always occupied the land. Like the cities of Umbria,
they are potent symbols of urbanity; and like these they become
more definite, more surprisingly crystalline to the mind, by reason
of the emptiness through which they are approached.

How much of the present susceptibility to these towns is
merely nostalgia, how much is pure hallucination, and how much
corresponds to a reality it is difficult to judge. Their buildings are
scarcely inhibited by either taste or culture, were improvised apparently without thought, seem to be the embodiment of a popular architectural consciousness, and present themselves to the eyes of the
present day as the final and the comprehensive monuments of an heroic age. But although it is by qualities such as these that Stein's
proposition is given substance, one hesitates to exemplify it by
them alone. These western mining settlements are after all too bizarre to prove a point. One recognizes in their buildings a peculiar
combination of good sense and outrage, of force and naïveté; but

one really demands that these characteristics be embodied in a more completely typical situation.

It is here that, as a quite stereotyped urban pattern, the American courthouse town might be introduced as a more representative illustration. A completely normal and widely distributed type, scattered throughout the northern states and consistently recurring throughout the South, it is scarcely the product of any deliberately expressed taste—and yet one assumes its repetition was inspired by more than mere habit. For patently this is a town dedicated to an idea, and its scheme is neither fortuitous nor whimsical. The theme of centralized courthouse in central square is—or should be—a banal one. And it is in fact one of great power. For these courthouse squares are not the residential enclosures of England, nor like the piazzas of Italy do they admit the church in a presiding role. Here it is the law which assumes a public significance; and it is around the secular image of the law, like architectural illustrations of a political principle, that these towns revolve. In each case the courthouse is both visual focus and social guarantee; and in each square the reality of government made formally explicit provides the continuing assurance of order (fig. 4). There is hence a curious decorum about these towns which, however run-down they might often be, are apt to display an air of generality. Urbanistic phenomena they palpably are, but they are also the emblems of a political theory. A purely architectural experience of their squares is therefore never possible. Within these enclosures the observer can never disentangle his aesthetic response from his reaction as a social animal. They are the foyers of a republican ceremonial, and their uncompromised form neatly condenses all the imponderables of republican principles. It is the almost classical typicality, the emblematic significance, and the completely adequate symbolism of these towns that is responsible for their seeming antiquity.

The place of origin of the type is presumably a matter of academic interest, but it is just possible that its place of culmination is in central Texas. There at least, since the comparative absence of trees disencumbers the scheme from camouflage, one can never be

Lockhart, Texas

4. Courthouses, Waxahachie and Weatherford, Texas.

TEXAS, PRE-TEXAS, CAMBRIDGE

unaware of it. Further west the central courthouse seems scarcely to have been a viable motif; but in Texas, where the brilliance of the atmosphere lifts the most modest architectural statement to a new potential, the idea becomes completely clarified; and for the unprejudiced eye, the eye which is willing to see, a number of small towns do present themselves as very minor triumphs of urbanity.

Llano, Lampasas, Gainesville, Belton, Georgetown, Lockhart, and others are all as much the same as so many French medieval *bastides*. If it is not the sight of a water tower, the first indication of arrival at one of them is apt to be the courthouse, which appears, from a distance of several miles, as the slightest eruption upon the horizon. Without major incident the landscape has unrolled itself for mile after mile with an almost complete negation of picturesque effect. Admirable, uncompromising, repetitive, restrained, monotonous, subtle, and unvaried, it is a scenically underfurnished and magnificently exhausting display which makes the minimum of overtures to the spectator. Without natural punctuation and without natural relief, it debilitates the eye; so that as an artificial caesura in an endlessly continued scheme the distant view of the courthouse acquires a peculiar significance. It is like a ship seen in mid-ocean—an evidence of amenity and a kind of monumental magnet which seems to impose progressive intricacy as the town is approached.

As a form of emotional complement to the interminable terrain, the impact of these four-square, geometrical, concentric little towns is discovered to be one of remarkable intensity. They have, all of them, something of the unqualified decisiveness, the diagrammatic coherence of architectural models; and scrupulously regular, they appear, almost more than real towns, to be small cities in primitive paintings. Something of their interest derives from their conformity, but within the accepted pattern innumerable variations are to be found. In one town brick will predominate, in another stone or stucco; in one place taste will be meager, in another elaborate; but in all of these places, as a common denominator of experience, there will be felt a dislocation of the sense of time. The buildings

Lockhart, Texas

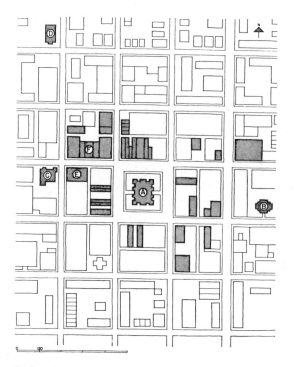

A. Courthouse

B. Jail

C. First Christian Church

D. St. Mary's Church

E. Vogel Block

F. Masur Block

5. Plan, Lockhart, Texas.

by which one is surrounded will appear to be ageless; while the insistently repeated courthouse and square will unavoidably suggest some Renaissance exercise to demonstrate the ideal significance of perspective.

As a representative of these towns at their best one might select Lockhart, whose exuberant, more than usually brilliant courthouse is apt to suggest that some provincial disciple of Richard Morris Hunt had discovered the irresistible fascination of Leonardo's studies for domical buildings (fig. 6). The first view of the town affords the characteristic visual competition. In approaching from the south the dominant intricacies of courthouse silhouette struggle for attention with the aluminum-painted spheroid of the water tower; and a concentration of interest upon either is further disturbed by the appearance to the right of a small castellated building, of curiously Vanbrughian profile. A toy fort, brick and machicolated; partly Romanesque and partly Italianate, evidently the jail, its disarming self-assurance sets the mood for the entire town (fig. 7).

As a preface to the architectural promenade of Lockhart this little jailhouse could not be more appropriate, and as one is led imperatively from it toward the square, it becomes apparent that expectations have not been raised too high. The courthouse is aggressive, bluff, and reasonably florid; the square itself is a more discreet combination of stucco, white paint, and Indian red brick, with here and there an intruding cast-iron column supplying a certain imported and Corinthian elegance. However, as one recovers from the shock of the square's central ornament, it becomes apparent that some of these minor buildings are not in themselves undemonstrative, and the presence of an interrupted staccato of distinctly assertive structures imposed upon the generally recessive background gradually becomes evident. It is particularly along the north and west sides of the square that these more individualistic buildings are concentrated (fig. 9), and especially at the junction of these two sides the presence of three white-painted gables of unequal height and width soon demands attention.

Lockhart, Texas

6. Courthouse, Lockhart, Texas. Alfred Giles.

7. Jail, Lockhart, Texas.

8. Library, Lockhart, Texas.

Lockhart, Texas

9. North side of courthouse square; Lockhart Savings & Loan Association on the northwest corner of the square.

From this northwest angle of the square another phase of Lockhart's architectural evolution is revealed. A short block lined by small commercial buildings leads to a church tower some three hundred feet away. The First Christian Church to which it belongs is as miniscule as the jail. An ecclesiastical representative of the Richardsonian suburban world of the eighties, dating from 1898, like the buildings on the square, it seems to have been put together from the standard elements provided by a box of bricks. But the First Christian Church is scarcely able to detain the observer, since three blocks down the street another disposition of church and spire presents itself.

This is St. Mary's, a product of Irish and German Catholicism, a building of orange brickwork relieved by brick of a yellow or deeper red and occasionally checkered, as for instance in the tower, with a pattern of greenish gray headers (fig. 10). St. Mary's is not so ambitious a building as the other; but its details are less ambiguous and more delicate, its modeling confident and distinguished, and its Gothic both lyrical and strangely firm, with something of the economy of a child's drawing of a church. It is with a shock that one discovers St. Mary's to have been erected in 1918.

The common sense of metropolitan time is severely jolted by this improbable fact. That this diminutive monument of unassuming piety should be nine years younger than the Robie House, should postdate Gropius's Werkbund Building by four years, imposes a sober curiosity which leads one to examine with deference the buildings already passed by. These, the structures immediately preceding the First Christian Church, are the Vogel Block to the south of the street and the Masur Buildings to the north. The Vogel Block is the first to demand attention (fig. 11). Dated 1908, invested by the heavy friezelike elaboration of its roof trim with a majestic seriousness, almost a floating prism, it seems to stand in a transitional relationship between the buildings in the square and those across the street. An awareness of a single volume, a sense of the horizontal, and a feeling for the significance of the structural bay are all emergent in the Vogel Block. In the Masur Buildings they have come to control the entire design.

Lockhart, Texas

10. St. Mary's Church, Lockhart, Texas.

11. Vogel Block, Lockhart, Texas.

The Masur Buildings (extending also along the adjacent
streets) represent the ultimate achievement in the commercial architecture of Lockhart. Erected at a variety of dates down to 1918, except for the Joe Masur Building (fig. 12), they are more avowedly
utilitarian than would earlier have been thought proper, and also
more classical. In them the episodic detail which characterizes the
square is no longer tolerated, the roof incident which still survives
in the Vogel Block is suppressed, and the only interruption of their
regular silhouettes is provided by the chunks of brickwork which
form a capping to the thin pilaster strips of their facades. The three
buildings across the street from the Vogel Block are large, simple,
and distinct units. Linked by one-story elements, they read as a
scheme of independent and varied pavilions, all manifesting the
new ideal of congruity, which is now seen to acquire a decisive expression in the last of the series, the Joe Masur Building. There, sub-
ordinated to a controlling grid of stringcourses and pilasters, in
simplified, almost abstracted, form, arches and all the acceptable
components of a classical design are fused into a single statement of
surprising intensity.

The three-floor hardware store, with all the consequence
of a small-town Italian palace, and the more fantastic Vogel Block
confront each other across the street with a certain defiant individuality. The First Christian Church occupies another corner. The
Catholic church is still in sight. And turning around, the perspective of the earlier buildings and of the north side of the square almost completes a survey of a series of apparently related structures.
It is not necessary to itemize their resemblances. They are in themselves a convincing argument of their relationship; and standing between them, their intrinsic reasonableness, their authenticity, their
unsophisticated strength, even their obvious weakness cause one automatically to presume the existence of some pronounced artistic
personality, some architect, or more probably, since this is not architects' architecture, some builder. This personality rapidly takes
shape, an unknown but not an indefinite figure, a master builder, a
Master of Lockhart, whom one equips with the attributes one feels

Lockhart, Texas

TEXAS, PRE-TEXAS, CAMBRIDGE

12. Joe Masur Building; northwest corner and south facade of Masur Block.

Lockhart, Texas

he should possess—an unsubverted integrity, an innate capacity, tastes which are uncomplicated and definite, an understanding of necessity. And for some moments—so strong is the light and so extreme the heat—the Master of Lockhart remains completely plausible.

But stubbornly, this ideally anonymous, quasi-medieval character whom one has educed refuses to take shape. The Master of Lockhart resists formulation as a myth. Indeed, was there one or were there several Masters? Was the architect of the Catholic church also the architect of the Joe Masur Building? Was the same man responsible for the Vogel Block and the jail? Apparently such questions are surprisingly difficult to satisfy and perhaps also they are irrelevant, because presumably it is the eternal problem of primitive art rather than the eternal problem of personality which is raised by these very recent buildings. They are structures which personally one finds deeply satisfactory; yet, with any conviction, one cannot attribute to their designer a developed or a conscious aesthetic intention, and certainly not the intention to produce the results of which one is most deeply appreciative. Seen dispassionately, these buildings are utilitarian structures casually enlivened by an elementary eclectic symbolism, deriving something of their effect from concentration and material uniformity. But it is now impossible and meaningless to dismiss them as this alone: in terms of a not unduly sentimental taste they have intrinsic virtues of a high order, while only too obviously their extrinsic attributes are even more telling.

Forty years ago, when the majority of them were new and some were still unbuilt, it was such a town as Lockhart that reduced the heroine of *Main Street* to an intolerable distress. "It was not only the unsparing, unapologetic ugliness and rigid straightness" which overwhelmed her, nor the fact that "in all the town not one building save the Ionic Bank" gave pleasure to her eyes; but it was buildings "crowned with battlements and pyramids of brick capped with red sandstone" which really promoted her dismay, and it was in place of these that "she saw a new Georgian town as graceful and beloved as Annapolis . . . or Alexandria." "She saw in Gopher Prairie,"

Sinclair Lewis tells us, "a Georgian city hall, warm brick walls with white shutters, a fanlight, a wide hall and curving stair. She saw it as the common home and inspiration not only of the town but of the county about"; and it was by fantasies such as these that she softened for herself the too harsh reality of a country which aspired "to succeed to Victorian England as the chief mediocrity of the world."

In the years that have intervened the neo-Georgian dream has receded, and as Victorian England has become less mediocre, so nineteenth-century America has become less abrasive. For many observers its towns have not yet become "as graceful and beloved as Annapolis," but their "rigid straightness" at least has become a positive value; while "their battlements and pyramids of brick" have become even more evocative than their English equivalents. They are now the indications of a self-consciousness as yet unimpaired by sophisticated inferiority or doubt, the distinguishing marks of a form of post-frontier architecture. It is a guileless architecture which, because innocent, is often apparently venerable; and which, because one may believe it to be uncorrupted, is sometimes curiously eloquent. When, as at Lockhart, it is combined with a city plan as entirely legitimate as that of the courthouse town; when, as there, a spontaneous and comprehensible architecture flourishes in a complementary relationship with a principle of authority; then we are in the presence, not of an amusing specimen of Americana, but of an exemplary urbanistic success whose meaning has been for too long obscured.

Lockhart, Texas

Transparency: Literal and Phenomenal, Part II

Written with Robert Slutzky, 1956; first published in *Perspecta*, no. 13–14 (1971)

An exhilaration with the light and the landscape of central Texas may still be as characteristic of persons newly arriving in Austin as it was in the mid-1950s, and Charles Moore once suggested so much to me. But forty years ago, when the Provençal dimensions of the Texas hill country could be added to the excitements of a new architectural curriculum, it was a highly volatile condition which ensued. It was a matter of Cézanne landscapes (with traces of Poussin) and an influence which then became hyper-stimulated by intimations of Synthetic Cubism and De Stijl.

Just a bit crazy? I suppose that it certainly was. However, it was in this condition of stimulus—landscapes and light, pictures and drawings—that Robert Slutzky and myself came to produce an article, "Transparency: Literal and Phenomenal"; and, about it, I can only say that, though the words must be mostly mine, the leading ideas must mostly have been Robert's.

For to my own naive arguments about Theo van Doesburg and De Stijl as interactive with Le Corbusier's Maison Domino Robert added a very big proviso. As a Fernand Léger and a Piet Mondrian man he insisted upon the assertive contributions of frontality and upon the supremacy of the picture plane. Or, in other words, he insisted upon statements of flatness as being provocative of arguments about depth; and, as I see it now, it was in this way that "Transparency" became an important private statement for what the Texas experiment was all about.

It was a dangerous and explosive little essay. It attacked the priority of sacred cows—most visibly that of Walter Gropius; and, being apparently insufferable, it also became unpublishable. Written in the fall of 1955 and sent to the Architectural Review *in London, it was not considered acceptable—by, I can only suppose, Nikolaus Pevsner; and, for him, it must have been almost total poison. In that peculiar Texas environment we had been encouraged to see too much and, as a result, "Transparency I" languished in obscurity only to be published nine years later through the good offices of Yale University in* Perspecta 8 *(1964).*

Nevertheless, in spite of immediate discouragement, Robert and myself still continued to strive (although Robert did not entirely approve of the results); but "Transparency II" enjoyed no greater success as regards any printing. Written in 1956, it was only published—again by Perspecta—*after a lapse of fifteen years! And, long before this time, of course we had given up all attempts at the third article which had always been planned. All the same there are themes deriving from "Transparency II" which recur in certain pages that follow, most evidently in "Giulio Romano's Palazzo Maccarani and the Sixteenth Century Grid/Frame/Lattice/Web" of volume two.*

In a previous article we elaborated, through a discussion of several Cubist and post-Cubist paintings, certain meanings which have attached themselves to the word transparency.[1] With the Bauhaus, Garches, and Le Corbusier's project for the Palace of the League of Nations serving as primary points of architectural reference, two kinds of transparency were investigated. They were distinguished as literal and phenomenal. Literal transparency, it was stipulated, could be experienced in the presence of a glazed opening or a wire mesh; but no definite conclusions as to the prerequisites of phenomenal transparency were presented. However, the examples of Garches and the League of Nations at least suggested circumstances which might be the cause of this manifestation; and thus it was implied that phenomenal transparency might be perceived when one plane is seen at no great distance behind another and lying in the same visual direction as the first. Consequently, it was further implied that among the causes (or, if one prefers it, the by-products) of phenomenal transparency there might be found a preference for shallow space or, where such space was not possible, for a stratification of deep space—so that the phenomenal as opposed to the real space could be experienced as shallow. But some of these suppositions are of so tendentious and so arguable a nature that in this present article it is proposed to consign them to temporary oblivion, and to concentrate attention, not upon the three-dimensional or spatial aspects of phenomenal transparency, but as far as possible upon its two-dimensional manifestations—upon phenomenal transparency as pattern.

Substituting the United Nations Building for the Bauhaus and Le Corbusier's Algiers skyscraper project for his villa at Garches, we might arrive at a parallel between the two former roughly approximate to the parallel which was maintained between the two latter. Thus the Secretariat of the United Nations may stand as a monumental example of literal transparency; and the Algiers skyscraper may represent almost a textbook example of that other transparency which Gyorgy Kepes defines as the capacity of figures to interpenetrate without optical destruction of each other.[2]

The published drawings of the Algiers skyscraper (fig. 13) show a tower whose organization may be apprehended in a variety of ways:

Transparency: Literal and Phenomenal, Part II

13. Project for an Algiers skyscraper, 1938. Le Corbusier.

1.   The eye may be engaged by the three horizontal bands which divide the structure into four definite areas.

2.   If these are overlooked or become recessive, the eye may become absorbed with the cellular pattern of the *brise-soleil,* and this pattern will gradually be felt to extend itself behind the horizontal bands.

3.   As the disruption of the *brise-soleil* pattern to the left of the facade becomes apparent, the observer will construct a further figure which, in mediating the two *brise-soleil* grids, appears as a kind of channel cutting open the facade and connecting the *pilotis* of the lower floors with the incidents on the roof.

4.   When this new figure is discovered to be interwoven with the three central floors of the building, the eye (or the mind) is compelled to provide further explanation and the observer comes to see the composition as a kind of E-shaped overlay imposed upon the "neutral" background provided by the *brise-soleil.*

These four variations are presented, not necessarily in the order in which they might be experienced, nor as excluding further interpretations to which they give rise, but simply with the object of establishing the basic figures whose presence a quite naive individual might detect.[3]

With the United Nations Building and the Algiers skyscraper as almost classic exemplars of literal and phenomenal transparency, it would surely be possible to sustain a classification of modern architecture according to the absence or presence of these qualities, but to do so would involve unnecessarily tedious analysis. The two interpretations which have been laid upon the word *transparency* become apparent from the comparison of these two buildings, and only in order to reinforce this distinction of meaning does it seem necessary to include a further parallel—one between Pietro Belluschi's Equitable Life Insurance Building in Portland, Oregon, and I. M. Pei's Mile High Center in Denver, Colorado (fig. 14).

TEXAS, PRE-TEXAS, CAMBRIDGE

14. Equitable Life Insurance Building, Portland, 1948. Pietro Belluschi. Photo by
Ezra Stoller. Mile High Center, Denver. I. M. Pei and Associates.

Transparency: Literal and Phenomenal, Part II

The former is evidently an instance of literal transparency. Direct, matter-of-fact, a kind of lucid academic critique of the Chicago architecture of the 1880s, it shows few of those characteristics which Kepes lists as those of (phenomenal) transparency. It barely exhibits either overlapping or interpenetrating figures, perhaps little contradiction of spatial dimensions; nor does it offer the observer a means of "simultaneous perception of different spatial dimensions";[4] and, except for its surface flatness, it is without equivocal meaning.

On the other hand, the Denver building, which displays a comparable regard for the structural frame and which is equally transparent in the literal sense, exhibits all of the foregoing ambiguities. Confronted with the Mile High Center, the observer perceives:

1. The vertical and horizontal gridding of a black structural frame.

2. A further system of gridding provided by a blue sub-frame which is constituted by the window mullions and the horizontal transoms or sill members.

3. That each of these frames provides a visual reinforcement of the other, and that their overlapping leaves some doubt as to where the floor levels of the building actually are to be found.

Further discrimination leads to the awareness that the black structural frame lies entirely in one vertical plane, and thus to the color black a specific spatial depth is attributed. Concurrently, an attempt is made to attribute a similar specific spatial depth to the color blue—only to reveal that the horizontal members of the blue sub-frame pass behind the black frame, while its vertical members pass in front. Hence, an equivocal contradiction of spatial dimensions results from this interweaving or overlapping of two figures which are simultaneously apprehended; and in order to explain this situation, first the black frame and then the blue will become dominant for the observer. At one time he will accept the existence of the blue frame in the two distinct spatial layers which it occupies, but at another he will seek to interpret its color according to the logic of color displayed in the black frame. Thus he will come to suppress the modeling of the blue frame and attempt to see it as entirely flat, but in doing so he will be obliged to see either the horizontal or vertical members of the black frame as pressed forward, or pressed back, or warped by the tension which has been introduced. This building is presumably an exceptionally succinct statement of a phenomenal transparency, but to certain types of mind the elegant post-Miesian achievement which it represents will suggest not only Chicago but also Italy. It is undoubtedly indiscreet to pluck such a building as the Farnese villa at Caprarola (fig. 15) from out of its cultural background and to propose that it may be examined face-to-face with this recent office building from Denver. The functions of the two buildings are not similar; their structural systems could scarcely be more unlike; the social context, the technology, the economy, the content which each implies can scarcely be related. But for the present we are concerned neither with function nor structure (as generally understood), nor with the social context, technology, economics, or content; but simply with the manifestations which reveal themselves to the eye.

Presented with one of the two identical garden facades of Caprarola, the observer recognizes a building organized in terms of two major stories, and he is quite shortly aware of:

1. The primary articulation of the wall which the orders and their respective entablature establish.
2. A further articulation of the wall which is effected by means of a sort of lattice of flat stone strips.

This stone lattice-work, which forms a visual insulation between the pilasters and the plastic activity of the windows, functions in two primary manners—as a subsidiary pilaster which serves the 'real' pilasters and confirms the vertical punctuation of the facade and as a frame which serves the bay, indicating a system of

15. Villa Farnese, Caprarola. Giacomo da Vignola.

paneling and providing the facade with a number of horizontal emphases of an importance almost equal to that of the lower entablature.

Thus the imposition of pilasters upon lattice leads (as at Denver) to an uncertainty as to the floor level and to an ambiguity as to the basic unit of the facade. By implication of the pilasters there are two major horizontal divisions; by implication of the projecting window heads below and window sills above, both of which may be read as lattice, a tripartite division of the facade is deduced. The overlapping and interlacing of these two systems and the fluctuations of significance to which each gives rise can pass without comment, for at Caprarola, as at Denver, it is apparent that the observer finds himself in the presence of an architectural tapestry whose warp and woof are immediately apparent to the eye but whose invisible threads his organizing instinct mentally reconstructs.

Now if Caprarola as well as Denver shows phenomenal transparency, we are obliged to conclude that, after all, it is neither a new nor even a post-Cubist manifestation; and perhaps if we were to trace back the evolution of literal transparency down the long route leading from the United Nations Building via such conspicuous monuments as the Bauhaus and the Crystal Palace to the great glass and stone cages of the later Middle Ages, we might also discover in these buildings some evidence of phenomenal transparency. In the nave of St. Denis (fig. 16), for instance, where the triforium rather than appearing as an independent unit will seem to be an intersection of the clerestory and the nave arcade, sometimes being subsumed within the first and on other occasions presenting itself as a projection of the second.

Thus almost any medieval or quattrocento Venetian palace will reveal similar attributes to a greater or a lesser degree, and the organization, although not the asymmetry, of the Ca' d'Oro (fig. 17) may be considered representative of the type. In the Ca' d'Oro a basically bipartite facade is presented, where one center is determined by the loggias to the left, and the other by the cutting of three

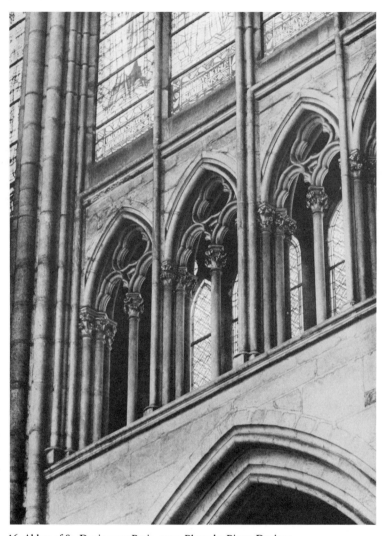

16. Abbey of St. Denis, near Paris, nave. Photo by Pierre Devinoy.

17. Ca' d'Oro, Venice. Photo by Osvaldo Böhm.

square windows through the plane of the wall surface to the right. Each of these two centers is invested with the control of sharply contrasted, clearly defined, and apparently symmetrical areas, which are isolated from each other by a thin, almost embroidered pilaster providing visual support for an heraldic trophy displayed on the second floor. But almost immediately after one recognizes this trophy, one proceeds to question it. It coordinates the space around itself and compels a symmetrical interpretation of the two windows between which it is placed, so that these windows are read together, and hence by means of this reading, the pilaster becomes, not the frontier between two opposed units, but the spine of an element straddling these units and demanding a revision of one's initial assumption as to the nature of each.

Once perceived, the uncertain valency of this pilaster quite undermines the primary response to the Ca' d'Oro facade; and, as the element which it has now produced receives further attention, this becomes even more problematical. Since it is symmetrical on the second floor, one is predisposed to believe this element to be symmetrical on the first; and when discovered not to be the case, when the two windows flanking the pilasters on this floor are discovered to be unequal, then further figural variations are automatically sponsored. Now, an attribution of symmetry to any one unit of the facade is discovered to be unwarranted, and each of the two major units acquires the ability to enlarge itself by absorbing this third; so that while the right-hand and left-hand sections of the facade are constantly augmented and diminished, infinitely more subtle relationships are now constructed, and, activating these, one might notice the schema provided by the rhythm of the projecting balconies and also the elaborate frilling of the cornice which, as a kind of arpeggio to the facade, provides a system of notation serving to intensify the polyvalent activity of the wall below. By these and other means, horizontal and vertical, L- and T-shaped configurations are finally precipitated within the intricate formal meshwork, so that first one element and then another comes to function as a kind of gear, the apprehension of which sets in motion whole systems of reversible mechanics.

TEXAS, PRE-TEXAS, CAMBRIDGE

87

The permutations inherent in a structure of this kind are identical with those which issue from less eccentric Venetian facades, and of these the sixteenth-century Palazzo Mocenigo (fig. 18) might be considered reasonably characteristic. Here, in a facade vertically divided into three, each division in itself is symmetrical, and the symmetry of each is reinforced in the center by triply repeated arches and in the sides by the elaborately mounted heraldic displays which are compressed between the windows of the *piano nobile.*[5] However, under sustained observation these apparently clear divisions of the facade begin to change. First, it is noticed that the central division enjoys the capacity to extend itself at the expense of the other two; and secondly, that the sides show a certain tendency to infiltrate, to slide in behind the outer bays of the central motif; while, following these initial realizations, the constituents of the facade enter into a successive series of relationships. At one stage the outer windows become isolated slots emphasizing the extremities of the wall; at another this same quality of slot is transferred to the central arched windows; and, presently, the heraldic trophies assume essential significance as the bonding element between these peripheric and central developments. At this stage the facade is dominated by a system of double H's; but, as its underlying structure becomes elucidated, this composition is displaced by a cruciform element which is implied by the plastic development of the principal floor and the association of the superimposed central arches. But the process of subtraction and addition continues, and as the upper and lower stages of the palace are now noticed to show a paneling of the wall, and as the *piano nobile* does not sustain the paneling, by this discontinuity of elements, another figure is raised into significance. Just as formerly the heraldic trophies effected a bridge between the center and extremities of the facade, now the central windows of the principal floor become the bridging element which integrates the two areas.

These different readings abstracted from the Palazzo Mocenigo by no means exhaust the possibility of still further ones; but they are in themselves a sufficient exposition of the functional multi-

18. Palazzo Mocenigo, Venice.

plicity with which each and every part of the design is endowed. Substantially the building is of Venetian origin; but the presence of certain features obliges one to presume the possibility of other influences also; and thus, on the top floor, because some Michelangelesque origin might be suspected for the profiles of the window pediments, one might also believe that something of the explicit nature of the overlapping and interlocking of figures derives from the same source.

Certainly in both the model and drawings of Michelangelo's proposed facade for San Lorenzo (fig. 19) everything that the traditional Venetian nuances of the Palazzo Mocenigo might obscure becomes clarified and exposed; and for this reason San Lorenzo requires little introductory comment. A wall surface modeled in low relief is articulated by means of a skeletal organization of columns and pilasters, by suites of mouldings, stringcourses, architraves, and a pediment.

So much is obvious; but it now becomes necessary to note the transpositions to which this skeletal organization proceeds to lend itself. Thus, to allow the eye to travel sideways across the design, four vertical elements—the coupled pilasters and columns—might be seen as contributing to the existence of a grid and as defining three larger spatial intervals (fig. 20a). But, almost immediately, this information is then subjected to 'correction.' These three spatial intervals, while they can appear identical in width, are, in reality, far from being so. The central is distinctly narrower than the flanking ones, and as a result, and in collaboration with the central pediment, a subversion of the initial reading is instigated. The inner sets of pilasters and columns now disengage themselves from the outer. They cease to participate in the apparent and 'neutral' grid. Instead they begin to appear as subservient to an hierarchical and centralized situation: and thus, in place of the quadripartite interpretation of the facade, there develops a tripartite division (fig. 20b). Likewise, if the eye travels up and down this surface there is something comparable which happens. Here to be noted is an elementary contrast between a low and a high relief. Columns below

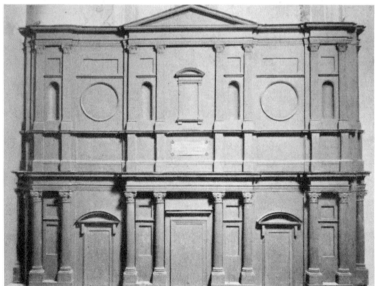

19. San Lorenzo, Florence: Michelangelo's sketch of his proposed facade, and a model done from this.

turn into pilasters above, and, thereby, a basic horizontal division becomes enforced (fig. 20c). But this, again, becomes an interpretation which cannot be sustained. The areas of emphatically high and emphatically low relief are separated by a contested territory (is it the attic to the one or the pedestal to the other?) which progressively insists upon its autonomy and which, accordingly, compels yet further revision (fig. 20d).

But so intimate and manifold are the interrelationships of figure which inhere within this organization that seriously to insist upon any initial or dominant interpretation is to be quite arbitrary; and therefore, rather than try to impose a private version of the continuous oscillations of appearance which San Lorenzo provides, it might be more expedient simply to allude to some of the more notable figures which it displays. These include:

1.　　A fluctuating series of H-shaped figures which are promoted by the intersections of the narrow bays and the 'attic-pedestal' (fig. 20e).

2.　　A further H-shaped figure provided by the lateral banding of niches, plaques, and central aedicule—'window'—in the upper wall, and by the equivalent banding and gapping of doors and panels in the lower wall (fig. 20f).

3.　　An expanding series of cruciform figures which are derived from the intersection of the 'attic-pedestal' and the central bay (fig. 20g).

4.　　A checkerboard reading which is created by three segmental pediments of the outer doors and of the upper 'window' (fig. 20h).

5.　　An inverted checkerboard which overlaps the preceding one and which is derived from the two circular plaques with their connected niches (fig. 20i).

6.　　A T-shaped figure generated by the impact of the pediment above and the high-relief development below which comprises some kind of reflection of the volume of the building lying behind and is presumably a residue of earlier studies (fig. 20j).

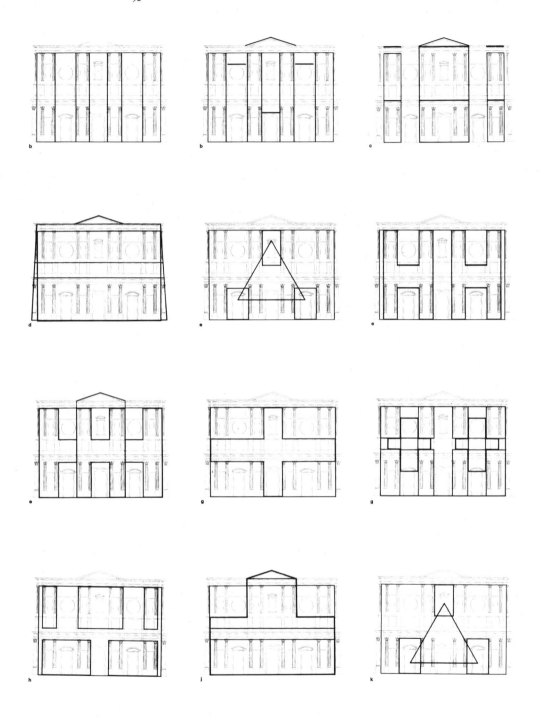

TEXAS, PRE-TEXAS, CAMBRIDGE

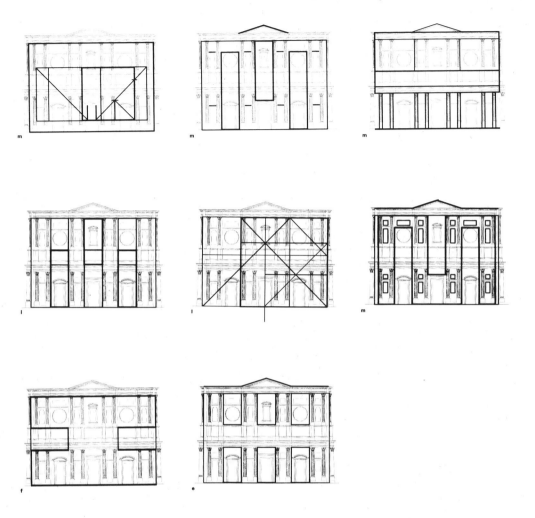

20. San Lorenzo: various interpretations of the facade.

A quite random observation of San Lorenzo discloses the immanence of at least such configurations as these; but a more discriminating examination can discover more concealed and subtle modulations. The segmental pediments of the upper 'window' and outer doors may again be noticed. These establish a triangle of interest: and, since the visual elements comprising this triangle are almost alike, there is a tendency to attribute to them a corresponding size. However, since one of these elements is smaller than the other two, there is a further tendency to assume it to be located at a greater distance from the eye; and thus, when seen in conjunction with the two doors below, the remarkable underscaling of the central 'window' (together with the understructuring of its immediate vicinity) introduces a curious tension between the readings of the horizontals and verticals in the wall plane. Providing an implication of depth, this underscaling suggests that beyond this vertical plane and visible through it there lies a perspective recession or an inclined surface to which each of these three elements is attached (figs. 20k, 20l).

With this last and almost Cubist transparency which Michelangelo has introduced, specific analysis of San Lorenzo need not be carried further. It should be apparent that these phenomena which we have examined are of an order closely comparable to those which we might find in many modern paintings—for instance in the later paintings of Mondrian; and although to erect a parallel between a Michelangelo facade and a Mondrian painting may at first appear as frivolous as a comparison between Caprarola and the Mile High Center, almost any representative of Mondrian's Boogie Woogie series might justify such a parallel. Thus, whoever chooses to examine with any care the incomplete *Victory Boogie Woogie* of 1943–1944 (fig. 21) will be obliged to extract from it a series of transparencies—of triangles, cross shapes, T's and U's which the composition may be said to spill over in a manner similar to San Lorenzo.[6]

Obviously dissimilar as regards their content and their more overt formal manifestations, both *Victory Boogie Woogie* and San

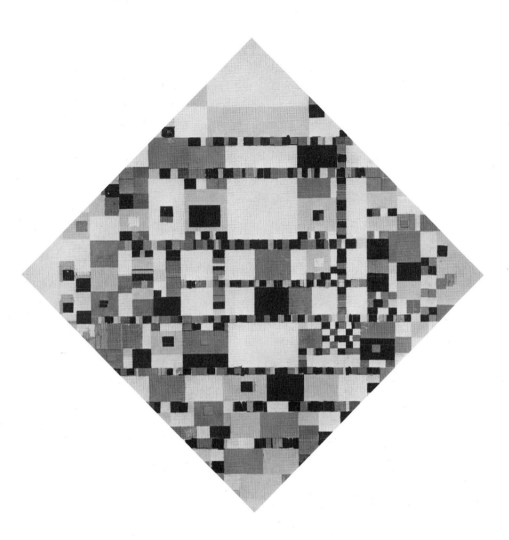

21. Piet Mondrian, *Victory Boogie-Woogie,* 1943–1944 (unfinished).

Transparency: Literal and Phenomenal, Part II

Lorenzo are at least alike in defying any accurate description of what they are. In San Lorenzo a lucidly symmetrical, monochromatic composition is saturated with alternative readings. In *Victory Boogie Woogie* an asymmetrical composition derives qualities of excitement from color, congestion, and the symmetrical nature of its individual parts. The readings of San Lorenzo are for the most part explicit; those of *Victory Boogie Woogie* are less expressed. The fluctuations of Michelangelo's facade are sudden; those of Mondrian's painting are less violent. In *Victory Boogie Woogie* the different areas of white gradually congeal to provide the central cruciform figure; and this figure slowly dissolves before a further interpretation in which the vertical axis provides a dominant element. But in both painting and facade there might be noticed a tendency of the different elements to build, to coordinate themselves, to amalgamate by means of proximity or common contour into larger configurations. Thus in *Victory Boogie Woogie,* while areas of red and areas of blue distributed throughout the canvas offer two alternative constellations, adjacent reds and blues show a tendency to withdraw from these systems and to unite into a series of larger wholes. In San Lorenzo these same propensities may be noticed. There, where a constellation of rectangular areas and columns and a rival constellation of circular and quasicircular elements are to be found, coalitions are constantly formed between the contiguous representatives of each system.

Again the facade and painting both show a disposition of frontally aligned objects which are arranged within a highly compressed space; both show these objects functioning as a series of relief layers for the further articulation of this space; and both show a framework syncopated by a staccato punctuation—in the one case of conventional architectural elements, in the other of small colored squares. In Michelangelo's design the wall plane which provides the mount, i.e., the 'negative' background upon which these individual elements are displayed, has the ability to assume an opposite role, i.e., to become in itself a 'positive' element or a series of 'positive' elements; and in Mondrian's picture one is conscious of the white areas behaving in the same manner. Thus in any primary interpretation of *Victory Boogie Woogie* the white rectangles will appear to designate a basic ground, a rear surface which supports the yellows, reds, blues, and greys; but, like Michelangelo's wall, Mondrian's white plane can cease to be recessive and, by exerting a pressure on the figures which initially it appeared to subsume, it can become as highly charged an element or series of elements as they.

By not permitting the eye to penetrate any far removed space, this rear plane prohibits a resolution of either composition in depth, and thus in each case its presence may be said to disturb the possibilities of central focus. In each case by investing the space of canvas and facade with a lateral structure, this plane functions as a generator of peripheric emphasis and replaces any one focal point by a series of differentiated episodes. By these means it acquires an overall surface tension, becoming a kind of tightly stretched membrane which acts upon the different elements it supports and in turn is reacted upon by them. Imbued by these elements with tautness, it presses them further forward; and thus, by reason of the spatial constriction which it creates, this rear plane serves both as the catalyst and as the neutralizer of the successive figures which the observer experiences.

Comparisons, parallels, and analyses such as these could be prolonged almost indefinitely, but possibly enough has been said to indicate the constancy of the manifestation which in contemporary works Moholy and Kepes have recognized as transparency.[7] In all instances their transparency—our phenomenal transparency—has taken place within a highly abstracted and intellectualized work of art; and in every case it has been the product of the most undeviating regard for formal structure, of the most remorseless and sophisticated visual logic. So much for the general context in which phenomenal transparency seems to appear; but for Moholy the transparency of meanings to which he responds in the writings of James Joyce is a method of building up a rich and manifold completeness. It is the literary analogue of the transparency revealed by Cubism— and this transparency, whether literal or phenomenal, is conceived by him to be a kind of symbol of space-time, which is mystically

Transparency: Literal and Phenomenal, Part II

validated by the discoveries of science and which, as a unique means of achieving cultural integration, is assumed to be inherent to the whole ethos of the twentieth century. But if there is any substance to the preceding investigations, then transparency is not the exclusively post-Cubist development which he supposed is independent of either modern physics or Minkowski; it is not characteristic of the twentieth century alone; and it has no necessary correlation with any impending integration of culture. In fact, almost the reverse could be claimed; and San Lorenzo, the Palazzo Mocenigo, Caprarola, at least, could be presented as the evidences of a Mannerist malaise, as the illustrations of "a self-conscious dissenting, frustrated style," as the indices to "a period of tormenting doubt, and rigorous enforcement of no longer self-understood dogma," as the external effects of mental disquiet, disequilibrium, schism.[8]

Now, that these two widely separated interpretations of closely related phenomena—the one insisting on the virtues, the other on the dubieties of phenomenal transparency—should exist side by side without any public embarrassment need not be hard to understand. In the first case, the mental block of so many Modern architects against history is notorious; and, in the second, the unwillingness of so many art historians to enter into serious criticism of contemporary achievement is one of the more patent limitations of that species. But if we can allow that in all the instances discussed, the method of raising fluctuating figures into ambiguous prominence is a common denominator which all share, then it becomes a matter of some urgency to know how, in the face of two such radically different evaluations of this common denominator, any justice can possibly be done to it.

One may of course propose that a common method of organization does not necessarily predicate an identity of psychic content; that the pursuit of phenomenal transparency may be sane, creative, and responsible (a received idea of Modern architecture); or that it may be deranged, capricious, and delinquent (a received idea of Mannerism); but if this proposition is unacceptable, then we are faced with a serious critical dilemma. The temptation is to escape it; and several attractive routes of escape do suggest themselves. Thus, we might, for instance:

1.   choose to deny the existence of phenomenal transparency as a visual manifestation;

2.   stigmatize the perception of phenomenal transparency as a product of hyper-aesthetic sensitivity or assert that its pursuit is no more than a formalistic side track of contemporary painting and architecture; or

3.   attribute a proto-modernity to Michelangelo, Vignola, and the rest or suggest that the contemporary architect who uses phenomenal transparency is Mannerist in spite of himself.

Escape route 1 is a congested road. Escape route 2 is a kind of spiritual autobahn which permits its travelers the pleasing illusion that in some sequestered cul-de-sac Picasso, Braque, Gris, Léger, Mondrian, and Le Corbusier are all involved together in some esoterically purposeless rite. Escape route 3 drags us on a sinuous detour through a linguistically picturesque terrain. The use of the first we might condemn as irresponsible and myopic; the use of the second we might dismiss as Philistine; while of the third we might say it is of no use. It is a kind of conquest of the problem by definition, that is, no conquest at all, for if we are at the liberty to attribute a proto-modernity—or a deutero-Mannerism—to all and sundry, then we make nonsense of the notion of modernity and whimsically subvert the categories of history. With all these escape routes ultimately closed, the problem therefore remains unilluminated, unsolved—at least in its wider implications. However, in its narrowest implications the mere existence of the problem at least suggests that phenomenal transparency does have a basis in common vision and does imply, on our part, some kind of archetypal response toward it.

In considering phenomenal transparency in this way, entirely at a perceptual level, it has not been possible to overlook Gestalt psychology, since the Gestalt psychologists, in their analysis of perception, seem to have been preoccupied with just those questions which are central to any examination of the problem. "Configuration," "figure-ground," "field," "common contour," "proximity," "constellation"—sometimes inadvertently and sometimes consciously our vocabulary has been saturated with the Gestalt phraseology, precisely because of the adequacy of its terms. Quite briefly, the Algiers skyscraper, the Denver building, Caprarola, the nave of St. Denis, the Ca' d'Oro, the Palazzo Mocenigo, San Lorenzo, and *Victory Boogie Woogie* look like some elaborate orchestrations of the rather curious little diagrams which are to be found so profusely scattered through any treatise on gestalt;[9] and, if in the presence of these diagrams we can overcome our primary amusement at what seems to be a discrepancy between a highly intellectual psychology of perception and its highly ingenuous visual examples, we might recognize these as exhibiting, in the most primitive form, the crucial circumstances which permit the development of the more complicated structures we have examined.

22. Figure-ground reading of a vase and/or twin profiles.

Thus, if we are not deterred by the combination of art nouveau and believe-it-or-not characteristics displayed by figure 22, it might be accepted as a representation of a basic figural ambiguity which has been consistently encountered. "Normally one sees a plain vase; it is only after a period of fixation that the profiles of two figures spring forth. What was once ground becomes figure and vice versa."[10] Similarly in figure 23 identical conditions are induced. One sees a black Maltese cross imposed upon a white octagon; but, by reason of the spatial quality of the eight constituent triangles, one's experience of this diagram inevitably reverses itself.

23. Maltese cross.

The possibilities of such "transfiguration" can be illustrated with rather more subtlety and perhaps with rather more direct architectural relevance (fig. 24): a group of rectangles is presented but "the figure may also be seen as two H's with certain intervening lines." These H's exist, but it is an effort to see them; and the figure in fact was set up by the Gestaltists to prove precisely this—that in spite of the existence of the H's, "despite our extensive past ex-

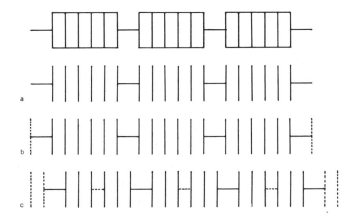

24. Various readings of a Gestalt diagram.

perience of the letter H, it is nevertheless, the articulation of the presented object (i.e., the rectangles) which determines what we shall see." [11]

But with certain minor modifications, the coexistence of the H's and the rectangles can become quite explicit, so that, in figure 24a, we are conscious of both. Here, by stripping off the top and bottom closures of the rectangles, the H-figures become completely exposed, but the rectangles themselves survive as unavoidable inferences which the observer constructs by reason of the identical length, proximity, and similarity of their ingredient elements. Preoccupation with the rectangles here leads to a fixation upon the four lines which constitute their horizontal axis; and, because of their identity of direction, ultimately these are seen as the visible parts of one continuous line which is presumed to pass behind a solid matter whose area concurs with that of the three rectangles. Thus, by reason of the breaking of this line, not only is an implication of depth introduced into a two-dimensional surface but also the presumption as to the existence of the rectangles receives confirmation.

Transparency: Literal and Phenomenal, Part II

In figure 24b, a further modification of the same figure, all of these activities become rather more manifest (fig. 9b). In this diagram the behavior of the horizontal lines becomes much clearer. The observer is either disposed to see four horizontal lines each of which functions as the crossbar of an H and is therefore led to complete two further H-figures; or, alternatively, he is led to see one interrupted horizontal line which appears as a split running through the middle of a background plane; but in each case, through an automatic interpretation of the presented object, he is led to provide it with a ground or to frame it within a field. Inside this field H's simultaneously function as the disengaging elements between dominant rectangles and also as the dominant figures themselves; while, as the observer's sensitiveness to the organization increases, it becomes apparent that minor rectangles must also be built up and that further H-shaped figures with double vertical members must be accepted (fig. 24c).

It is not necessary to say more in order to demonstrate the applicability of this last diagram to the facade of San Lorenzo or to that of the Algiers skyscraper; it is equally evident that the kind of perceptual activity which this diagram involves is of the same order as that which is exercised at a much higher level, with longer periods of fixation, in a painting by Léger or Mondrian; and in all these cases the figure-ground phenomenon which is exemplified may be said to be the essential prerequisite of transparency.

According to Gestalt theory, while figure is generally seen as figure by reason of its greater closure, compactness, density, and internal articulation and while ground is generally seen as ground by reason of its lack of these qualities, in the figure-ground relationship the ground, although it may at first appear anonymous, is neither subservient nor passive. As an environment imposing a common relationship on all that happens, it is also an enclosure containing figures which it lifts into prominence; and these, by reason of the prominence with which they become endowed, react upon the ground and provide it in turn with a figural significance. There is thus in figure-ground a double function inherent to each of the components. Each can be itself and its opposite; so that any specific instance of figure-ground is a condition of being of which the components are at once the product and the cause, a structure which becomes significant by reason of reciprocal action between the whole and its parts, and—one might say—an area of reference, qualified by and at the same time qualifying the objects which are referred to it.

In complicated examples of figure-ground such as those we have examined, the ground obviously contains several figures, and these in themselves also function as subsidiary grounds supporting further configurations. Gestalt maintains that the observer organizes these discrete visual stimuli according to certain laws, which are stated as factors of proximity, similarity, direction, closure, experience, "good curve," "good gestalt," "common fate," "objective set," and the untranslatable *"Prägnanz."*[12] "Gestalt theory," it is stated, "does not hold that the senses carry amorphous material on which order is imposed by a receiving mind" but attributes powers of discrimination to the senses, refusing "to reserve the capacity of synthesis to the higher faculties of the human mind" and emphasizing instead "the formative powers," "the intelligence of the peripheral sensory processes." In other words Gestalt conceives the act of perception not as a simple stimulus-response reaction but as a process which might be characterized as follows: "Constellation of Stimuli—Organization—Reaction to Results of Organization."[13] Further, Gestalt supposes that mental activity and organic behavior are subject to the same laws, "that 'good shape' is a quality of nature in general, inorganic as well as organic," so that "the processes of organization active in perception somehow do justice to the organization outside in the physical world."[14]

But supposing the senses are endowed with 'intelligence', with powers of discrimination, with organizing capacity; and supposing physical and psychical processes to be governed by the same rule. In themselves these hypotheses really seem to have very little to do with what appears to be the inordinate Gestalt interest in phenomenal transparency, which it recognizes under a variety of names as "phenomenal identity," "double representation," and "duo formation."[15] One is apt at first to consider this interest to be no more than a reflection of an intellectual style which has characterized the first half of the twentieth century, to regard it for instance as parallel to the critical literary interest in ambiguity disclosed by such studies as William Empson's *Seven Types of Ambiguity,* to the art historical interest suggested by the reinterpretation of the sixteenth century, to the artistic interest implied by analytical cubism and so much of Modern architecture. But although the preliminary Gestalt researches into figural ambiguities do date from the years during which Analytical Cubism made of phenomenal transparency a principal method of composition, it must be recognized that something of the Gestalt 'taste' for figural ambiguities is related to its emphasis upon field.

For Gestalt the existence of a field is a prerequisite of all perceptual experience. Consciousness of field, it is assumed, must proceed consciousness of figure; and figure in itself is inconceivable in isolation. In this article attention has been directed toward visual fields alone, and Gestalt does seem to have favored visual illustration of field; but obviously field as such must vary with the nature of the objects and/or perceptions involved. For instance, in the case of our apprehension of a tree, the field may be provided by a mountain, or a lake, or the wall of a house, or any number of things; in the case of our apprehension of a poetic metaphor—in itself a field—the larger field may become a sonnet; in history a given epoch may endow with 'field properties' the idiosyncrasies of the various figures which it supports. But in all these cases the field is assumed to be more than the sum total of the elements which it embraces. Genetically it is prior to them. It is the condition of their quality and the reason for their behavior.

It may now become possible to see that the Gestalt interest in ambiguity is not merely arbitrary. The unstable, equivocal figure-ground phenomenon, whose fluctuations may be either sluggish or volatile, brings the supporting matrix, the field, into high prominence. Figure-ground is figure-field keyed up to a pitch of maximum contrast. It is field revealed as positive; and thus for Gestalt it is the ultimate summary, the classic condensation of the field idea.

Notes

1. Wilhelm Fuchs, "On Transparency," in W. D. Ellis, ed., *A Source Book of Gestalt Psychology* (London, 1938), 89.

2. Gyorgy Kepes, *Language of Vision* (Chicago: P. Theobald, 1944), 77.

3. "Intervention of the plastic sensibilities. All seemed to be implacably controlled by the succession of rational requirements. The plan was rigorously symmetric. But by a further tracing of the Golden mean the posture of the facade has become asymmetric. The form seems to swell to the left then shift to the right. It is responding to the double call of the site, the cliff, the sea." Le Corbusier and François de Pierrefeu, *The Home of Man* (London: The Architectural Press, 1948). It is in these terms that Le Corbusier describes the fluctuating figures which the Algiers skyscraper provides.

4. Kepes, *Language of Vision,* 77.

5. It is interesting to notice that the facade of the Palazzo Mocenigo (a refacing of an older medieval structure), although symmetrical in all its parts, is not in itself symmetrical.

6. The diamond is a result of a rotated square whose diagonals, formerly tending to be read as vectors inducing recessional perspective, now become an ideal right-angle armature stiffening that plane and investing the points, rather than the edges, with the capacity to act as terminals to the scanning eye. In this performance, a 'gravity-free,' buoyant, and thoroughly frontalized plane is established exerting pressure from behind to any chromatic figuration placed upon it.

7. László Moholy-Nagy, *Vision in Motion* (Chicago: P. Theobald, 1947), 350; Kepes, *Language of Vision,* 77.

8. For these quotations see Nikolaus Pevsner, "The Architecture of Mannerism," in *The Mint* (1946), 132, 136. They may be regarded as reasonably representative of a received idea.

9. Kurt Koffka, *Principles of Gestalt Psychology* (New York: Harcourt, Brace and Company, 1935); Wolfgang Kohler, *Gestalt Psychology* (New York: H. Liveright, 1929); George W. Hartmann, *Gestalt Psychology* (New York: Ronald Press Company, 1935); Ellis, *A Source Book of Gestalt Psychology.*

10. Hartmann, *Gestalt Psychology,* 25.

11. Ellis, *A Source Book of Gestalt Psychology,* 58.

12. See Wertheimer, "Laws of Organization in Perceptual Forms," in Ellis, *A Source Book of Gestalt Psychology,* 71.

13. Hartmann, *Gestalt Psychology,* 100.

14. Rudolf Arnheim, *Art and Visual Perception* (Berkeley: University of California Press, 1954), 73.

15. "Phenomenal identity," Ellis, *A Source Book of Gestalt Psychology,* 147; "double representation," Koffka, *Principles of Gestalt Psychology,* 178; "duo-formation," ibid., 178.

Review: *Forms and Functions of Twentieth Century Architecture* by Talbot Hamlin

Written 1952; published in *The Art Bulletin,* 1953

My review of Talbot Hamlin's book is a Yale piece proposed by Russell Hitchcock and it involves most of my preoccupations of that period, 'composition' and 'character'. I find it relatively intelligent and, as I have intimated, crucial for Texas; but at the same time, I remain mildly shocked by what, nowadays, I would call its naive Hegelianism.

The four volumes of Mr. Talbot Hamlin's treatise follow a logical and a traditional sequence. In the first, he is concerned with the Elements of Building—the functions of certain rooms, circulation, simple structure, landscaping, and interior design. In the second, he discusses Principles of Composition—the abstract ideas of proportion, scale, rhythm, character, and style, which are followed by a further analysis of structural systems. The third and fourth volumes contain discussions of individual building types contributed by experts in each subject. In the preparation of the work Mr. Hamlin has acted as coordinating editor, but the responsibility for the book in its final encyclopaedic form must also be that of the editorial board appointed by Columbia University.

In his preface to the work, Dean Leopold Arnaud of the Columbia University School of Architecture outlines the motives which inspired its preparation. Briefly, a need was experienced for a new work to succeed the last great synthesis of academic theory, Guadet's *Eléments et théorie de l'architecture,* published in 1902. It was felt that the present day, with its recent experience of new structural types, new programs, and new ideas of form, required a collation of this kind; and that, since the main lines which future development was likely to follow had now been laid down, such a review could aspire to legitimate authority. Since this new work is envisaged as a successor to Guadet, any criticism of it must revolve around two questions: Have the editors succeeded in providing a new work which replaces Guadet? Was the provision of such a work necessary? Before attempting to answer them, it will be desirable to make some preliminary attempt to assess Guadet's significance.

Julien Guadet (1834–1908), the architect of the Hôtel des Postes in Paris, a student of Labrouste at the Ecole des Beaux-Arts and subsequently a pensioner at the Villa Medici, was from 1871 onward a teacher, and from 1886 professor in the Theory of Architecture at the Ecole. In succession to J. N. L. Durand's *Précis des leçons l'architecture,* Guadet's treatise, the record of his lectures, established itself as the internationally accepted summation of academic architectural doctrine, and his four volumes lay down much the same outline that Mr. Hamlin's follow. Guadet's experience, both as an architect and as a teacher, obliged him as a theorist to accept the validity of an eclectic position. In attempting to rationalize such a position, he was obliged to pursue his researches beyond what were assumed to be the transitory aspects of stylistic form, in order to reveal the underlying elements on which it was conceived that all good architecture has, at all times, been based. By this method, he was able to isolate as factors of primary importance certain functional, structural, and aesthetic principles of organization. By this same method, he was also able to rise above the necessity of mere stylistic judgment, and to evaluate the architectural product, not as the emanation of a given historical period, but in terms of a permanent value, as the embodiment of continuously present, underlying, and rational principles.

Guadet's justified success is indicated by the large number of subsequent publications which appear to have been derived from his work. In America and England alone, the treatises of such architectural professors as John Vredenburgh Van Pelt of Cornell, John F. Harbeson, Nathaniel Cortland Curtis of Tulane, Ernest Pickering, and Howard Robertson were at least partially inspired by Guadet's example; and it is not an exaggeration to state that during the first third of the twentieth century, in some degree or another, Guadet's rationale was endorsed by the curriculum of every architectural school in the English-speaking world.

Both Guadet's virtues and his defects arise from his background as a Frenchman, as a pupil of Labrouste, and as an eclectic. By virtue of the French tradition he is endowed with the confident authority of unchallenged academic scholarship, and by reason of his personal relationship to Labrouste he is led to place great emphasis on structure. Drawing on the French feeling for ingenious commodity in the organization of rooms, he envisages the plan as the essential generator of architecture, and it might be claimed to have been his influence which elevated the plan to that position in contemporary architectural theory which has been continuously affirmed by Le Corbusier.

By reason of his eclecticism Guadet is unable to confirm that primacy which Labrouste gave to structure. He finds Labrouste's definition of architecture as "the art of building" incisive but incomplete, valuable in its time as a manifesto, but defective by its failure to emphasize the importance of composition. Guadet, it would seem, by a catholicity of taste hoped to achieve a comprehensiveness which was lacking in Labrouste's theory. Envisaging all centuries and countries as a reservoir of possible motifs of composition,

Review: *Forms and Functions of Twentieth Century Architecture* he is able to deduce certain broad conclusions, to discover in all periods the presence of a common denominator which is conceived of as transcending style. This—the presence of effective composition supported by appropriate character—is his standard of judgment, and the stylistic framework within which this ideal is realized becomes for him a matter of only minor consequence. Thus, implicit in Guadet's treatise is the idea that, at all times and in all places, the architect's motivation is purely rational and formal. Unable to comprehend the internal individuality of particular styles, he is also unable to explain the phenomena of historical differentiation. Able by reason of his criteria to explain *appearance,* he is not able to explain the intimate and irrational preoccupations on which appearance is based. Affirming ideas of stylistic reminiscence, but indisposed to attribute a compulsive urgency to style, Guadet's method ends by destroying the logic of the historical process, while insisting on the value of historical precept.

    Eléments et théorie de l'architecture may be considered as the major instrument of certain important architectural traditions of empirical thought and eclectic practice. These traditions have not been without their influence on the evolution of a specifically Modern architecture; but, judged from the standpoint of the mid-century, Guadet's work now appears involved in precisely the historical situation above which it sought to rise—it belongs irrevocably to the years around 1900. Having satisfied the material requirements, Guadet envisages an architecture of pure form; but an architecture in which the element through which form is made manifest, the element of style, is purely a matter of taste and personal bias and so, in the last degree, an irrelevance.

    Basically, the problem of Guadet's significance raises that of the aesthetic and the ethical descent from nineteenth century theory. The school of universal eclecticism which Guadet represented has never passed without challenge. In France the pure tradition of rationalism, elevated to a program by the neo-Grec school and amplified by Viollet-le-Duc, has continued to claim adherents; in Germany those attitudes derived from Schinkel and Semper have consistently represented an opposite conception; in England convictions as to the ultimate value of the Gothic Revival theory of Ruskin have never been completely extinguished; while in America the school of Louis Sullivan and the example of Chicago indicate at least one powerful attitude of dissent.

As a whole, the proponents of this second architectural theory, the ethical or moral tradition, claim the adherence of the Modern movement. In the mid-nineteenth century conviction that authentic architectural form can be generated only by a respect for the physical ingredients of material and structure, Modern architects perceive the historical antecedents of their own attitude. This conviction is conceived as defining forms of indisputable integrity, so that an architecture generated from such a basis is believed to possess an objective significance which is denied to forms ensuing from the mere exercise of visual preferences.

Thus stated, these generalizations wear a falsely simple air. Parallel schools of thought cannot exist without continuously modifying each other, and rarely in practice does a theoretical position emerge with complete doctrinal clarity. In spite of frequent protestations to the contrary, the Modern movement has consistently shown the most highly developed interest in form for its own sake; and in spite of its aestheticism the eclectic tradition, too, has been obliged to accept something of the contemporary ethical interest.

It is hardly necessary to add that Guadet has never been among the heroes of the Modern movement; that his association with the Ecole des Beaux-Arts has always been sufficient reason for historians of Modern architecture to ignore his existence. That he did contribute a valuable, and to some extent a creative, pedagogical discipline seems to be proved by experience; yet it can hardly be denied that his relationship to the Modern movement is a wholly ambiguous one.

Guadet's treatise has survived into the present day with diminished prestige, so that the attempt to provide a new summation of architectural theory is understandable enough. As Dean Arnaud observes: "Guadet's book, destined for European architects of fifty or sixty years ago is woefully inadequate for twentieth century designers who must cope with new methods and new problems and must create types of building that did not then exist. The systems and aesthetics current today were just beginning to take form at the end of the nineteenth century and except in the work of a few individuals were so embryonic as to be scarcely recognizable."

From this quotation it will be perceived that the problem of evolving an adequate theoretical treatise to replace Guadet is twofold. The importance of new structures and new programs must be asserted, and the range of new forms which they permit must be completely exhibited. At the same time, the significance of new "systems and aesthetics" must be made absolutely clear.

But in the same paragraph Dean Arnaud also tells us that "the basis of architectural composition is unchanging and holds good in the present as it did in the past"—a dictum which, if not so diffuse as to be without critical value, appears explicitly to deny the possibility of any new aesthetic, or indeed of any historical evolution at any time. Here we find the first of the contradictions in which *Forms and Functions of Twentieth Century Architecture* abounds. It becomes clear that in the minds of the editorial board the central tenet of eclectic theory remains completely valid. The assumption of a visual common denominator behind all architectural experience passes completely undisputed. The specific experience of a modern aesthetic remains effectively blanketed.

Further study of the first two volumes merely reinforces any suspicions provoked by this preface. "New methods and new problems" are described; new "systems and aesthetics" scarcely receive the most cursory notice. The reference of the editors to Guadet is now perceived to be far from accidental: their book is another *Elements and Theory of Architecture* and not, as its title suggests, an evaluation of specifically twentieth century forms. Guadet's aesthetic continues to be the criterion of selection, and from the publication of fifty years earlier the new book derives both its weakness and its strength.

The work itself falls into two parts—the first two volumes are largely a discussion of principles and their abstract application, the last two comprise a series of statements of the factual requirements of various building types. No single reviewer could attempt a survey of these last two volumes, in which individual articles contributed by experts on particular building types demand separate criticism from equally informed sources. The entire range of building programs, from the individual house to the whole complex of the city, receives exhaustive treatment, and each section is provided with a very complete bibliography. This section of the work will probably be the one most frequently consulted, but it is likely, as different building types receive new interpretation, that these two volumes will require the publication of supplements to keep them up to date. These discussions of specific programs are considered to lie beyond the scope of this review, which will be concerned with the content and implications of Volumes I and II.

Accepting the fact of this work's relationship to Guadet, both in concept and content, it remains to be seen what meanings and significance it possesses for the present day.

Mr. Hamlin achieves a most comprehensive presentation of the functional requirements of various building elements. His description of different structural methods is lucid, and he succeeds in indicating quite clearly the role which structure has always played in architectural expression, but he has neglected to provide an adequate treatment of the increasing influence of prefabricated and standardized parts upon architecture. He is perhaps at his very best in his discussion of planning and of the interplay of plan and structure. Here the ideals of the French academic tradition thoroughly inform his observation. He has all the French sense for effectiveness of parti, all the Beaux-Arts feeling for the plan as an architectural counterpart of the musical score. It is significant that among Modern architects Le Corbusier should have consistently shown the most developed feeling for the formal possibilities of the plan; and while one could not claim for him any direct relationship with the Ecole des Beaux-

Arts, the mere fact that the spatial material of Modern architecture should have achieved its most rational crystallization within a French milieu is sufficient to indicate that here Mr. Hamlin's contribution is of immediate importance. In his analyses of the integration of function and structure, in his discussions of sequence and climax, in his instinctive awareness of the inflections and jointing of the plan, Mr. Hamlin is able to present a critique which few architects trained exclusively in the framework of the so-called International style could provide.

For the presence of these virtues the eclectic descent of this treatise must be responsible, but by reason of this same descent it is upon the rocks of architectural composition that Mr. Hamlin founders. Composition has been laid under something of an embargo by the Modern movement; the word hardly occurs in the vocabularies of Le Corbusier and Gropius. We need not inquire into the reasons for the inhibitions surrounding its use, since it is apparent that although Modern architects may not care to employ the term, any process of organization is still one of composition. The principles of architectural composition which Mr. Hamlin outlines are substantially those which have been affirmed by all eclectic theorists since Guadet; and are conceived as applying, irrespective of stylistic motivation, to buildings representative of widely differing cultures, like the Temple of Khons at Karnak, Canterbury cathedral, and the Palazzo Massimo. Throughout this discussion it is assumed that the basis of composition is unchanging, and while it can be understood that with Guadet the necessity to rationalize an eclectic position could lead to a thesis of this kind, the same necessity does not exist today. Were the same thesis to be applied to a discussion of painting, the student would presumably learn that, say, both Sassetta and Guercino had observed the same principles of composition, and that this common denominator was equally applicable to other cases so diverse as Monet or Hokusai.

This conception of eternal principles of composition has become a truism in academic circles—though at any time before the late nineteenth century it might have evoked some surprise. It can hardly be believed that such principles correspond either to historical knowledge or to contemporary experience, and it might be surmised that they represent no more than a reduction of late Baroque and neo-Classical compositional schemes, a simplification of these schemes in terms of the direct effect demanded by a painterly vision. If this is so—and the principles of architectural composition are certainly a fairly recent discovery—then this doctrine appears as no more than an *a posteriori* academic formula in terms of which, about 1900, it came to be assumed that all good buildings were evolved.

Preoccupied with the principles of composition, neither the author nor the editorial board of this treatise seem to have enjoyed any direct experience of the compositional schemes which derive from Cubist painting by way of Constructivism and the Dutch De Stijl group. Mr. Hamlin reproduces two paintings by Mondrian and comments on their significance for such architects as J. J. P. Oud and Mies van der Rohe; but he does not seem to be aware of how radically Mondrian's system of composition differs from all previous examples, nor how catalytic in the evolution of Modern architecture was van Doesburg's influence in the early 1920s. He fails completely to make clear how absolutely opposed were the compositions of De Stijl and Constructivism to the principles of Guadet and his generation.

The ideal of composition as it was understood around 1900 was a concentric one, implying generally a grouping of elements about a central space or void and a downward transmission of weights according to a gravitational scheme. Against these principles De Stijl advanced what was called "peripheric" composition, developed not toward a central focus but toward the extremities of the canvas or wall plane and involving, in a building, not a gravitational but a levitational scheme.[1] The influence of this formal experiment upon Modern architecture has often been denied, but it cannot be overlooked that every historically important architect of the 1920s was affected by it; and all the major monuments of the time, from Les Terrasses at Garches to the Bauhaus and the Barcelona Pavilion, embody in some degree the results of this discovery.

Review: *Forms and Functions of Twentieth Century Architecture*

When Gropius writes in 1923 of "a new aesthetic of the horizontal . . . which endeavours to counteract the effects of gravity," he states quite clearly the levitational idea; and when he adds that "at the same time the symmetrical relationship of parts of the building and their orientation towards a central axis is being replaced by a new conception of equilibrium which transmutes this dead symmetry of similar parts into an asymmetrical but equal balance," he recognizes the significance of the peripheric scheme, although he provides a different explanation for it.[2]

Absorption with Constructivist form has perhaps diminished as the 1920s have become more remote, but it has never ceased, in some way or another, to be part of the central tradition of Modern architecture. Peter Blake makes quite clear how Constructivism has continued to provide a major discipline for Marcel Breuer;[3] in contemporary Italian development it is clearly the dominant formal impulse; and although in the new Harvard Graduate School and the Unité d'Habitation at Marseilles its influence may be less immediately obvious, the inflections and rhythms which were liberated by De Stijl are still palpable.

No theory of contemporary vision is possible unless these developments are taken into account. Nor are they explicable in terms of the aesthetic of Guadet and the eclectic school. Mr. Hamlin has taken too literally the Modern movement's characteristic protest—that it is without formal preference. He conceives Modern architecture to be precisely what so many architects have declared it to be—exclusively a process of rationalization. He has been unwilling to assert what so many suspect—that Modern architecture is a style, as legitimate and as limited as any of the great styles of the past.

Mr. Hamlin rejects Le Corbusier's definition of style as "a unity of principles animating the works of an epoch, the result of a state of mind which has its own special character." Such a definition, however broad Mr. Hamlin may find it, at least establishes the fact of style as a historical concept; it recognizes at any given moment in time the existence of an animating unity of principles. Mr. Hamlin prefers to restrict style to a "coherence both inner and outer, both of factual arrangement and artistic expression"; in fact, he conceives style as little more than consistency, and is thus able to arrive at the conclusion that style derives from a "unifying ideal," which may be "one of delicacy, of eloquence, of power, of strength, even of economy or of efficiency." With Mr. Hamlin, style is purely a personal and a psychological matter, restricted to specific occasions and conditions and apparently lacking in general implications. "Style," he tells us, "is not unrelated to character," and indeed his conceptions of both somewhat overlap.

Character in architecture Mr. Hamlin finds to be both an objective and a subjective quality, corresponding to his factual interpretation of style as coherence and to his psychological interpretation of it as expression. Character in building provides, in the first instance, "an intellectual picture of what goes on in it"; and, in the second, "proper character can come solely through the expression of the appropriate human emotion which the building should arouse." Earlier commentators, Guadet and Curtis, noticed that the demand for character was a comparatively recent development. According to Guadet:

> La recherche du caractère est d'ailleurs une conception relativement moderne. L'antiquité a bien des édifices nettement caractérisés, mais elle ne parait cependant pas avoir fait du caractère un mérite capital. Ainsi le Parthenon, temple de la divinité athénienne, et les Propylées, porche militaire d'une citadelle, présentent les mêmes éléments; de même les salles des thermes et la basilique de Constantin.

Guadet's statement could be confirmed by a reading of Rudolf Wittkower's *Architectural Principles in the Age of Humanism,* which would suggest that character in architecture was not among the interests of the Renaissance either. The idea was of course bound up with the individualistic tendencies of Renaissance humanism, but the characteristic does not seem to emerge as an isolated and definable concept until the late eighteenth century. The Renaissance, stressing the ideal and the universal, concerned that its buildings should exemplify archetypal patterns, was indisposed to examine the particular situation and comparatively disinterested in purely local, characteristic circumstances. The old opposition between the typical and the characteristic has possibly lost much of its significance, but it still serves to define certain categories of the mind, and it might be questioned whether Modern architecture, any more than that of the Renaissance, recognizes a problem of character. The aspiration toward a classical impersonality, the search for the standard, for the anonymous, are not ultimately compatible with the impulse toward characterization. In Marcel Breuer's words, the Modern movement seeks "what is typical, the norm; not the accidental, but the definite *ad hoc* form";[4] and while this may or may not be a matter of regret, Mr. Hamlin should have made clear that the presence of expressed character has not at all times been considered a prerequisite of good architecture.

In his discussions of both style and character Mr. Hamlin has in no way advanced from an eclectic apologia. If style is exclusively a matter of coherence, then, so long as it respects its materials and is well detailed, the coherent *pastiche* of a Louis XVI chateau possesses style. If character is the expression of appropriate human emotion, then, so long as it achieves a degree of functional representation, the most spurious play on the optic nerves is justified by its psychological effectiveness. In both these chapters (nos. 9 and 10 of volume 2), *Forms and Functions of Twentieth Century Architecture* is at its weakest. With his interpretation of character as little more than expression, and style as entirely a personal quality, Mr. Hamlin makes a misnomer of his title and renders his work of selecting representative material almost impossible. He notices that only after generations "can we begin to pick out from the complexity of structures produced by a civilization those common elements which are the hallmarks of its style." This no doubt is true, as is his observation that the use of the word "style" is "a hampering influence rather than a help to the designer." But to select the Customs House at New Bedford, Massachusetts, as an illustration of "style resulting from materials," from "granite detailed to express its strength and natural origin," is less than half the explanation of a building in which the most unpracticed eye can detect the predominant influence of the internationally diffused neo-Classical ideal.

Mr. Hamlin's unwillingness to involve himself in historical judgment is linked with his unwillingness to investigate the specific unity of principles which animates the architecture of the twentieth century. In the last analysis, the authentic process of artistic creation is also unconsciously a critique of history, the intuitive recognition that at the moment of creation only a limited range of possibilities can claim a real legitimacy. It is the positive statement of what, for a given occasion, is historically significant that causes the manifestations of Le Corbusier and Gropius still to survive as the classic statements of Modern architecture's aims. Here where creative tension is at its highest, the animating unity of principles is scrupulously observed. Here, instinctively and without any thought of style, but by means of a positive position with regard to history, style is formed. Like all style, it is dynamic and perpetually evolving, but it is not the "stylishness" of particular buildings or designers. It is rather the super-rational expression, the abstraction of preoccupations which are organic to our society. Mr. Hamlin is confident that "the historical style of the twentieth century is being inexorably developed . . . by many forces—economic, sociological, industrial, political," that "we are expressing our culture, whether we will or no; just because we are architects living at a certain time and in a certain place," but he is not willing to go further. He examines results but not motivations, and from a reading of this treatise one might think that the twentieth century style is being defined largely by external pressures, since so little attempt is made to define its internal, specifically architectural initiative.

For these reasons, Mr. Hamlin's choice of illustrations of representative buildings will strike many of his readers as strangely unbalanced. The buildings and projects which many have come to consider formative are often unduly neglected. There are, for instance, no less than thirteen illustrations of the State Capitol at Lincoln, Nebraska, and none of the Bauhaus. The Pavillon Suisse receives no more than two small line elevations; and so considerable a document of contemporary planning as Le Corbusier's project for the League of Nations Palace is illustrated by a block plan, an elevation, and three perspectives so small as to be almost unintelligible. Among distinguished architects of an older generation, Gropius receives perhaps the most cursory treatment: a unit plan of housing at Siemenstadt, Berlin, two illustrations of housing at New Kensington, Pittsburgh, and two photographs of a factory at Greenwood, North Carolina, are presumably considered adequate indications of the work of a man whose immediate influence has revitalized the architecture of the North American continent. Of the members of a younger generation, Marcel Breuer's work receives neither reference nor illustration; Giuseppe Terragni, Franco Albini, and the contemporary Italian school pass equally unnoticed.

It is disappointing that this work, upon which so many distinguished names have collaborated, should leave behind so incoherent an impression. The example of Guadet was perhaps too much in the minds of the editorial board for them to function with complete independence, and in the restatement much of his disciplined directness of thought has been lost. To provide academic formulae for contemporary architecture is a very understandable objective, but this effort, which is possibly premature, demands something more vital than the reiteration of a fifty-year-old apologetic. Much of Guadet's doctrine remains completely valid, but much demands a more stringently selective analysis than it has received so far. Modern architecture has rather more profound implications than this book envisages. In 1902, *Eléments et théorie de l'architecture* was a historically cogent work. Its successor of 1952 could have been equally significant had there been a greater realization of the essential reasons why Guadet had become "woefully inadequate."

Notes

1. Cf. *De Stijl* (Amsterdam: Stedelijk Museum, 1951).

2. Cf. *Bauhaus* 1919–1928 (New York: Museum of Modern Art, 1939).

3. Peter Blake, ed., *Marcel Breuer* (New York: Museum of Modern Art, 1949).

4. Ibid., 119.

Review: *Roots of Contemporary American Architecture* by Lewis Mumford

Written 1954; published in *Architectural Review*, 1954

This is a piece proposed by the Architectural Review. *Written in Austin while I was scribbling with Bernhard Hoesli, it must also represent those travels which I had made around the U.S. in which, believe it or not, I had visited some fifty Frank Lloyd Wright houses.*

The European architect must often feel that much of what he sees illustrated as the Modern architecture of the North American continent bears as little relationship to the architecture which he envisages as the buildings of McKim, Mead and White, in their time, bore to those of the Renaissance. American buildings seem rarely to be carried to a state of three-dimensional conclusiveness and not often to be the results of extreme aesthetic effort. They are lacking in tension, they are without the purely formal virtuosity which typifies so much European endeavour, they are usually diagrammatic rather than developed. But such critical scruples apart, it remains beyond doubt that in the mid-century the North American continent offers the most adequate and comprehensive laboratory for the study of contemporary architecture. Unlike the European achievement of the 1920s and '30s this is not an architecture of isolated masterpieces. There are no Garches, no Pavillons Suisses, the ratio of major monuments to total production is low, but where unremarkable Modern buildings abound they are presumably endorsed by popular taste, and with its revolution completed, Modern architecture, universal and unnoticed, has ceased to be a manifesto and become simply architecture.

Whether or not this is a happy state of affairs is entirely a matter of preference, but it would seem that Americans have very well known what Europe has partly forgotten—that quality, apart from being a personal achievement, is also an attribute or result of quantity. What Modern architecture in America has lost in plastic finesse, it has gained in physical perfection; what it has lost as a sophisticated art of private meaning, it has gained as the symbol of a communal vitality. It is for these reasons that any publication on American architecture must enjoy a particular significance, and it is an explanation of this situation that one turns to Lewis Mumford's recent book. Unfortunately his title is hardly a sufficient indication of its contents.

Roots of Contemporary American Architecture is in fact an anthology of thirty-seven essays dating from the mid-nineteenth century onward, which are assumed to represent the principal critical traditions synthesized in the architecture of the present day.[1] Arranged under seven headings, the first three groups of essays illustrate the continuing influence of the mid-century romantic-rationalist school, the emergence of regionalism, and the recognition of an aesthetic based upon the machine. The fourth is concerned with the architectural achievement of Chicago, while the fifth and sixth rather loosely comprise discussions of domestic architecture and the architect's social responsibilities. His seventh group Mr. Mumford has entitled "The Search for the Universal."

Drawing largely upon contemporary documents, this book becomes, as its editor says, a documentary history of ideas, and believing that the individual essays present a self-explanatory sequence, he has attempted to confine his role of interpretation to a minimum. In doing so one might doubt whether he has been strictly fair either to himself or to his reader, since, however much interpretation may be abjured, it is present by inference in the actual choice of material, and despite his professed editorial aloofness it is clear that Mr. Mumford's material is selected so as to illustrate a point of view.

A first turning over of this book suggests that he has been too concerned to find for Modern American architecture an immaculate and wholly correct ancestry; and one may be pardoned for doubting whether anything so vigorous and demonstrative as this architecture has shown itself to be could have emerged from antecedents of such unfailing respectability as those which these essays establish. The intellectual circles from which the contemporary American architectural conscience is allowed to be derived seem a little too well accredited to justify the healthy aberrations which from time to time it has displayed; and the overwhelmingly Puritan genealogy which is here proclaimed scarcely explains that unreserved and expansive self-confidence which typifies so much building activity in America.

This insistence upon wholly ethical origins has the effect of setting up a frame of reference, which while it facilitates criticism does so by the elimination of historical texture and contemporary paradox. It substitutes a mythology of Modern architecture for a rationally convincing account of its evolution. Such a mythology, in which the extremes of eclectic depravity are sharply and cleanly contrasted against an architecture of high moral tone, very certainly has its place, but it has been too frequently publicized to be received yet again without embarrassment.

The constructions of later criticism have perhaps overclarified the account of Modern architecture's origins, and it would seem that part of the value of publishing contemporary documents might

Review: *Roots of Contemporary American Architecture*

have been in their reestablishing something of the *density* of history
which a too partisan analysis has eliminated. After all, Modern architecture is now sufficiently old to be able to examine even the Ecole
des Beaux-Arts with some degree of objectivity, and particularly
where critical tabus have gathered thick, as around the discussion of
the Chicago Fair, the notices of responsible visitors might have permitted a partial reassessment of a still unexplained architectural
volte-face. It is for instance difficult to believe, as we are constantly
asked, in the calculated apostasy of a whole generation of mid-
western architects. It is equally difficult to believe that Chicago's
collapse in the face of academic invasion could have been so
ignominious and complete if its architects had possessed the intellectual vigour and self-consciousness which is nowadays attributed
to them. Louis Sullivan's remarks are no doubt still the best summary of the fair, but it would have been interesting to have learned
how so clairvoyant an observer as Frederick Law Olmsted explained
his participation. A spectacle of architectural decadence, the fair was
a major event as regards city planning, and paradoxically what appears today as aesthetic irresponsibility seems to have instigated a
pattern of urbanistic order which supplied many American cities
with what are still their finest deliberately organized visual effects.
Distressing though these facts may be, their consequences cannot be
overlooked in considering contemporary American architecture, and
it would have been only just if in this anthology there had been included some contributions by representatives of the City Beautiful
movement.

It is in such a case that this collection appears most completely as the reinforcement of an already somewhat worn historical
stereotype, but since Mr. Mumford is concerned with illustrating
the development of a creative nucleus of ideas, such criticism is
not completely relevant: his criteria of selection do not lie in history
but rather in his conception of the American architecture of the
present day.

Mr. Mumford is one of the most sensitive critics of the
world we see about us; he has been one of the most energetic, sin-

cere, and completely devoted apologists of Modern architecture,in both the United States and Great Britain; a twentieth century Ruskin, he has educated a whole generation to the understanding of his enthusiasm and the appreciation of his prejudice. At some time all have experienced his influence and have emerged from it with a more developed perception, but the immensity of his achievement should not obscure the fact that his overwhelming interest has never been so much in great architecture as in a just social order, and from the apparently vanished age of liberalism he has retained the conviction that the presence of the second will automatically secure the first. Such may still be a fundamental belief of the Modern movement, but if so, it becomes progressively less tenable, and in this case it leads Mr. Mumford to a preference for perpetually embryonic form. It causes him to condemn Le Corbusier for his historical innocence, to find the origins of Cubism in America, and to discover superlative architectural values in redwood.

Presented through the medium of these essays the contemporary American architectural scene becomes altogether too much a matter of cosiness and aspiration. One fails to recognize in it that vast, diversified, and noisy theater, constantly and indiscriminately stimulated by technological change. One sees nothing of that plenitude, that superabundance of reasonable quality. One looks around for the big operators, the neo-academicians, the lunatic fringe. One perceives dimly the outlines of the empire of Mr. Wright, one looks around in vain for indications of that rival Chicago empire of Mies van der Rohe; but Mies and (more surprisingly) Gropius have been neatly kept off the stage.

No exposition of contemporary American architecture can claim to be complete where there are such omissions. It is a sign of the receptivity of American building that it can absorb, utilize, and systematically develop personalities so divergent and opposed: and it is a sign of its aesthetic nerve[2] that it can permit distinct architectural schools systematically to approach culmination. In purging the American scene of its complexity, in subduing its competitive glitter, Mr. Mumford has presented only half a picture, and his subject, incomplete, is also denatured.

Review: *Roots of Contemporary American Architecture*

128

He has not been led to this interpretation by any narrow ideological significance attached to the idea of a specifically American architecture. He is on the contrary convinced that architecture in the United States is most significantly American when part of a worldwide community, but apparently he is not willing to allow this community to be one of idea. Rhetorically enquiring as to what is the American tradition in architecture Mr. Mumford offers the equivocal assertion that it is the Modern tradition, and reading on it becomes clear that 'the Modern tradition' at its most profound is a matter of practical empiricism informed by transcendentalist sociology. One has elsewhere been led to believe that Modern architecture does possess a dogmatic core, and it is not easy to accept, as Mr. Mumford infers, that an architecture which is preoccupied with intellectual concepts is no more than a brittle formula, without, as he says, "the qualities of a living art . . . at best a mask or a form of scenic decoration."

A practical empiricism, such as Mr. Mumford endorses, may do "justice to the timebound, the local, the living and the subjective, and therefore the unique and the finally incalculable," but, however high-minded it may be, having no essential reference to a body of ideas, ultimately without the power of abstraction, it is lacking in the capacity to coordinate or crystallize. As a student of sociology and politics, Mr. Mumford is anxious to eliminate from the artistic process its formal result, and with him the consequences of artistic creation, rather than a successive series of completed states, seem to become the analogy of biological evolution. An intellectualism such as Mr. Mumford condemns necessarily ends in sterility, but a simple pragmatic individualism such as he apparently approves, by destroying the possibilities of knowledge, ends also in destroying the individual, since it removes his capacity to know himself.

Obviously both attitudes are necessary, and the real becomes no less so and the ideal is not vitiated when they confront their opposites. Attitudes of deduction and induction, commitment and skepticism, dogma and doubt, fortunately for the critic or analyst, are essential components in any situation for it is out of these antitheses that any valid historical criticism must emerge, and by eschewing conflict Mr. Mumford makes Modern American architecture no more than a series of well-meaning intentions. It is intolerable to believe that any achievement so authentic could have been prompted by origins so sentimental and diffuse, and it is hard to assume that we are expected to understand it to be so.

Or is it indeed the case, and is this yet again the critical dilemma with which America seems always to provide its most sympathetic admirers?

Notes

1. Lewis Mumford, *Roots of Contemporary American Architecture* (New York: Reinhold Publishing Corporation, 1952).

2. "Aesthetic nerve" or "aesthetic verve"? In my text I had written "nerve" but as published by the *Architectural Review* this became "verve." Strange that the turning upside down of just one letter should so radically alter connotation! In returning the proofs of this piece to *AR* and to Reyner Banham, then copy editor, I made a point of how an *n* had been changed to a *v;* but, rather strangely, the *v* still persisted.

Cambridge 1958–1962

Written 1994

It must have been in 1961, perhaps in October, that I made a little dinner for Clinton Rossiter and for Peter Eisenman, at that time my neighbor living just around the corner. Clinton Rossiter had just come from the history and government department at Cornell to spend a year at Cambridge teaching as Pitt Professor (I imagine something like political theory); and it must have been because he was still in the grip of an original mystification and surprise that his conversation that evening exuded a peculiar brilliance. Apparently he needed a sounding board to relieve his culture shock, and, presumably, Peter and I were able to supply this.

Thus, the colleges of Cambridge were "no more than the Potemkin villages of education"; and while the mere idea of the Empress Catherine sailing down the river—not quite wide enough for the purposes—with her lover displaying a succession of academic false facades was something of a joy to entertain, he still went on. The university itself, he said, should get a different name. Not the University of Cambridge, it really should be called Fenland Tech; and we should all go out and get T-shirts to advertise this message.

But he had just returned from a brief visit to Oxford and it was this which produced the punch line of the whole evening: "To leave Oxford for Cambridge is like leaving an overblown but neglected rose garden for a horticultural research station in the wilds of Siberia."

So, if I didn't necessarily agree with his details, I still applauded his state of mind. The supercilious blandness of Cambridge, all that *nil mirare* stuff, had disconcerted *him* just as it had disconcerted me three years before.

So how and why did I come from Texas to Cambridge?

After the collapse of the Texas experiment those associated with it felt themselves to be somewhat at a loss; and this was particularly so with reference to John Hejduk, Robert Slutzky, and myself. But, thanks to John Hejduk, I spent some time at Cooper Union and, thanks to Howard Barnstone, some time at the University of Houston before accepting a position as visiting critic at Cornell for the academic year 1957–1958. But meanwhile (and this thanks to Sandy Wilson), negotiations had already begun with Sir Leslie Martin, who had recently been appointed head of the School of Architecture at Cambridge; and there were rumors (which I believed) that this was going to lead to a *great* reform.

It was for these reasons (still more Texas melodrama?) that I sailed from New York in the early summer of 1957 to take another look at Cambridge. I sailed on a Belgian freighter called the *Lualaba* after the river of that name in the Congo (now called Zaire); and, for what it is worth, it might be noticed that, at that time, there was a Belgian line with all of its ships named after the rivers of the Congo—the *Luapala,* the *Lukuga,* the *Luindi,* the *Lufira.* Based in Antwerp, it operated a version of the old slave trade triangle—from Antwerp to the Congo Belge (was this the present day port of Banana?), from the Congo to New York (in order to allow the rich *colons* a little bit of shopping—Saks Fifth Avenue, Bloomingdale's, Altman's, Henri Bendel, etc.?), and from New York back to Antwerp. In other words, restricted to twelve passengers, the maximum that a freighter was allowed to carry, it was a little trip that promised social diversion and, maybe, useful information; and it certainly supplied it.

Thus, in mid-Atlantic one was certainly encouraged to anticipate that dissolution of the Belgian colonial empire which was shortly to occur; and, arriving in the Channel, one was compelled to witness what *had* been the historical basis of English power. Ships approaching the port of New York are never sluiced into such narrow waters; but here there was an incredible congestion of traffic making a former English prerogative quite clear—the power to close the ports of Hamburg, Rotterdam, Antwerp, etc. at almost a moment's notice. And so, all that day, we steamed up the Channel, with Ostend to the right in the early afternoon, with the Scheldt in the late afternoon—and here it was that our elevation above the meadows caused everything and everybody, whether cows or women, to look like something out of Rubens, heavy and sumptuous—to dock in Antwerp just as it was about to become dark.

Allowed to land the next day, one walked around Antwerp to the usual places, the cathedral and the house of Rubens. I had been there before; but all this was now to be seen with a different eye. An American eye it happened to be, but just as well it might have been French or Italian. Still foreign Antwerp appeared—but, after Texas, was it not strangely familiar? Indeed was not that smallness of everything and that profusion of detail no more than an illustration that Antwerp, Hanseatic Antwerp, had always been an annex to London?

The idea did *not* please me but, all the same, it was not to be eradicated; and, after I had taken a train to the Hook, I could only feel that I was being serviced by London Passenger Transport, that I was approaching England by the backdoor, that Belgium, Holland, and London were all part of the same landscape of the mind.

From the Hook of Holland to Harwich, from Harwich to Liverpool Street, I arrived in London to find myself in the presence of *some* thing about which Belgium had already provided the clue. It was an architectural aberration thought to be normative. I was confronted with a wilderness of quoins and columns, with an outbreak of architectural prolixity quite beyond the relatively innocent imagination of Antwerp, with the prospect of the miniature and the mea-

Cambridge 1958–1962

ger elevated to the status of an 'imperial' event; but I still thought that I must be wrong, that—in some way—my eye must be diseased. And, being so, being determined to give London a try, in the belief that more protracted exposure might be a palliative for instant exasperation, I set out on a long walk.

I walked from Liverpool Street to Charing Cross, and from Charing Cross to South Kensington, before I sat down and was obliged to recognize that though I was attempting to alleviate a supposed disease of the eye, I still found London more than *outré*. All that Edwardian rustication, all of those columns never to be found in Rome, all of those Palladian windows never to be found in Venice[1] had simply acted not to help my eye but further to exacerbate my mind; and it was in this way, though our terms of reference were very different, that I sympathized with the arguments of Clinton Rossiter several years later. He and I had both experienced a bad shock, which related to miniaturization, to claustrophobia, and to excessive proliferation of detail. As regards myself, I had seen all this in visual terms—as a miniaturization of building and spatial enclosure; but, as regards Rossiter, I can only think that he must have seen it as a quite dreadful accumulation of related social subservience all to be observed in the typical structure of a Cambridge college.

But not to go on in this way. Against the promptings of common sense I was allured by Cambridge, and there I spent four years.

They were profitable-unprofitable. I was mildly stimulated but, for a year, I must have written in a vacancy. But I still wrote quite a lot, private scribbling in default of any public animation.

However, in 1960 this was changed by the arrival of Peter Eisenman, from Cornell-Columbia and Jacquelin Robertson from Yale-Oxford-Yale; and, thenceforward, with the exception of a piece on La Tourette, it was conversation that usurped the role of writing.

Note

1. See Rudolf Wittkower, "Pseudo-Palladian Elements in English Neo-Classical Architecture," *Journal of the Warburg and Courtauld Institutes.*

Le Corbusier: Utopian Architect

First published in The Listener, *February 12, 1959, this short article derives from a radio discussion on the BBC's "Third Programme" of very shortly before, and it bears all the signs of having been written almost overnight. It is republished here partly because of the engaging naïveté of its concluding sentence, which is in the sharpest contrast with the conclusions of my article "The Architecture of Utopia" of only a few months later (Granta 63, no. 1187 {1959}).*

In any case, this represents my last overture from the BBC.

It is often well to begin with a text, and a quotation from Wyndham Lewis's *Time and Western Man* may provide a sobering commentary, either before or after a visit to the Building Centre in London to see the current exhibition devoted to Le Corbusier. Wyndham Lewis wrote:

When a great creation or invention of art makes its appearance, usually a short sharp struggle ensues. The social organism is put on its mettle. If it is impossible quite to overcome the work in question, it is (after the short sharp struggle) accepted. Its canonization is the manner of its martyrdom. It is, at all events robbed of its effect by a verbal acquiescence and a little crop of coarse imitations. Nothing really ugly or powerful, in most instances, has been at all disturbed.

The earlier decades of this century did indeed witness a "great invention" of art, and the authority of this "invention" is made beautifully clear by Le Corbusier's achievement. Was it perhaps a foregone conclusion that society could not resist the rebellious simplicity of the programme which informs all his activity, so that, after a show of resistance, it was accepted and a revolution was thus completed? For the success of any revolution is also its failure. Initial demands are never perfectly satisfied; while, in terms of specific objectives, concrete results will always appear as a corruption of original principles; and thus today Modern architecture may be felt to have become all that it was never intended to become. For it was an architecture which was sustained by the faith that it was to change the world, to regenerate society and, in short, to redeem mankind. And except for provincial pockets of resistance it is now as successful as any architecture is every likely to be. It is patronized by governments and endorsed by great corporations. It is established. It is orthodox. It is official art. And thus, rather than the continuing *symbol* of something new, Modern architecture has recently become the *decoration* of everything existing.

Perhaps we may be relieved that this is so. But our feeling of relief in itself constitutes the central irony involved in any appraisal of Le Corbusier today. For his plastic achievement as presented at the Building Centre can scarcely be separated from his ideology, and fundamental to Le Corbusier's ideological position there is the expectation of a Utopia, his belief that salvation is to be expected through architecture. Given the Ville Radieuse, given a planned world, he constantly seems to reiterate, then everything will be set right. Justice will be just and politics moral; while "tourism, leisure and work will find fluidness, charm, utility."

Between the real calamities of the century and this engaging vision there is a gap which daily becomes more glaring; and there is therefore a certain pathos which attaches itself to this large exhibition of Le Corbusier's work. The millennium, on the possibility of which so many of his principles were predicated, seems now to be infinitely remote; while in the retrospective, precedent-ridden climate of the present his highly abstracted idea of society and his single-minded commitment both seem to belong to an age entirely lost beyond recall.

But it is in the nature of genius to override or to dismiss the probabilities of a given historical situation; and in this way—by discarding the merely probable and by proposing the apparently impossible—Le Corbusier has been able to effect a genuine renewal, so that paradoxically it is only now when his basic faith has come to seem incredible that his formal influence has reached a zenith. Almost wherever we are likely to go we shall come across imitations (and imitations of imitations) of his work; while, in his ability to provide a quarry of source material for his professional contemporaries to mine, he has possibly been surpassed by no other architect since Michelangelo.

His influence has been principally exercised through the medium of the illustrated book; and if we wish to understand its nature, it is to his early treatise, *Towards a New Architecture,* and to the publication of his buildings and projects as his *Oeuvre Complète* that we must look. For in these books he evolves a frame of reference, persuades us to accept it, poses the problems, and answers them in his own terms; so that, like the great system makers of the Renaissance, Le Corbusier presents himself to us as a kind of living encyclopaedia of architecture, or as the index to a world where all experience is ordered and all inconsistency eradicated.

Le Corbusier: Utopian Architect

But if the world of Le Corbusier may be said thus to answer to emotional necessity, it is not for all that a completely harmonious one. In his scheme of things, the intellect is obliged constantly to oscillate between polar extremes. On the one hand, looming very large in his mental life, there are the Parthenon, the Pantheon, the forum of Pompeii, the Grand Court of the Louvre; and, on the other, looming no less large, there is something which he calls "the engineer's aesthetic," a matter of aircraft, Canadian grain elevators, old steamships, the roof of the Fiat works in Turin, low-pressure ventilating fans, Bugatti engines. In other words it is perfectly simple, though perhaps a little too simple, to propose that Le Corbusier's architecture is the product of a dialectic between the Mediterranean classical tradition and certain technological achievements of the early twentieth century which are conceived of as being preeminently 'modern'. Like earlier exponents of the classical tradition, Le Corbusier does believe that there are truths which are true for all time and ideas which are independent of place; and, accordingly, very much like Alberti or Palladio, he aspires to discover these principles, that "axis of organization which must indeed be that on which all phenomena are based," which "leads us to assume a unity of conduct in the universe and to admit a single will behind it." And if in passages of this kind Le Corbusier's classicizing bias is so pronounced that he can almost sound like someone paraphrasing Alexander Pope's *Essay on Man,* it is not surprising that for him, as for earlier representatives of the same mental family, architecture should be largely an affair of elementary geometrical solids and simple mathematical ratios. "Geometry is the language of man," and looking for further proof of this Le Corbusier attempts to bring this idea of unchanging principle into relationship with the facts of a changing technology. He does so by proposing that techniques based upon special knowledge are closer to his "axis of organization" than art based on mere caprice; and thus he is able again and again to ram home virtually the same idea: that "Engineers produce architecture, for they employ a mathematical calculation which derives from natural law." In some ways here again we might still feel ourselves to be in the eighteenth century, but surprisingly it was by classical ideas such as the law of nature (which prompted lyrical excursions into the world of the machine) and it was with only subsidiary gestures towards the spirit of the age that Le Corbusier enlivened architectural polemic more than thirty-five years ago. It was a rigorous debate between past and present that he sometimes seemed to propose that architecture should become, but it was as a somewhat different debate that his own achievement developed.

In most of his works the classical component is there simply as a preference for highly abstracted volume, though there is a further ingredient perhaps of a specifically French classicism in the extraordinary strictness of some of his spatial distributions. But, as is very well known, and as the present exhibition provides evidence to illustrate, it was particularly Synthetic Cubism which formed the real catalyst of his style, and almost all his buildings have been simply the consequences of bringing together the compositional method of Cubist derivation with a somewhat generalized conception of reinforced-concrete structure. Thus the drawing of 1915, showing the reinforced-concrete skeleton of what he called the Maison Domino, constitutes the datum for almost all Le Corbusier's activity [see fig. 2]; and it is characteristic of his turn of mind that he should have proposed such a structural method as being suitable for a small house. But it is in reality more a necessary idea which he here presents than a necessary structure. It is, one might say, an idea which Le Corbusier has deduced as being the solution to the problem *architecture;* and it is therefore a controlling idea from which for many years he was not disposed to deviate.

It is understandable why. The resolution of the building into simply columns and horizontal planes offered a remarkable accommodation for formal ideas of Cubist origin; and thus Le Corbusier was able to create an apparent amalgam of the two of such vigor that the rest of the world has really been unable as yet to think of any other. Seemingly he was the first to grasp the idea that a structural organization of this kind, with its absolute equality of rhythmic punctuation and its sandwich-like layers of space, acted to prohibit any centralization of emphasis. And seemingly he was the first consistently to apply an opposite principle of emphasis—that of distributing important episodes not in the centre but around the edges of the building. Drawing on the continuous Cubist experiment with exactly this type of 'peripheric' composition, by allowing a variety of planes to enter into a contrapuntal relationship with the concrete skeleton Le Corbusier was able to strengthen intrinsic characteristics of that skeleton, and he was able to do it in a way which was so convincing that his creation almost encourages an illusion that the reinforced-concrete frame and the Cubist discovery were complementary manifestations. This achievement has been Le Corbusier's chief contribution to architecture, but it is a contribution which he himself has developed and enriched with a consistency of which none of his competitors have been capable. For, borrowing again from the methods of Picasso or Braque or Léger, he has been able to elevate the accidents of the modern metropolis to a pitch of aesthetic relevance, to draw them into his scheme of things, and to make of them the elements of a significant architectural orchestration.

But, though he has derived so much from the study of the city, his own urbanistic achievements are scarcely to be considered to rank alongside his architectural ones. All of his buildings were for many years thought of by him as parts of a city, a city which was later to be fully realized; but this city of the mind of which, say, the Swiss Pavilion is an important fragment, though it has a formative significance for so much of his activity, and though it serves to rationalize so many of his innovations, was never charged with any of the brilliant spatial stimuli which the assumption of its existence helped to produce in his individual buildings; and consequently one may well be left wondering whether this Ville Radieuse was ever a serious proposition or whether it was not simply a necessary mental convenience providing him with a closed field in which activity could be isolated and raised into prominence.

In a "Third Programme" discussion last week, entitled "Le Corbusier and the Future of Architecture," the nature of his town

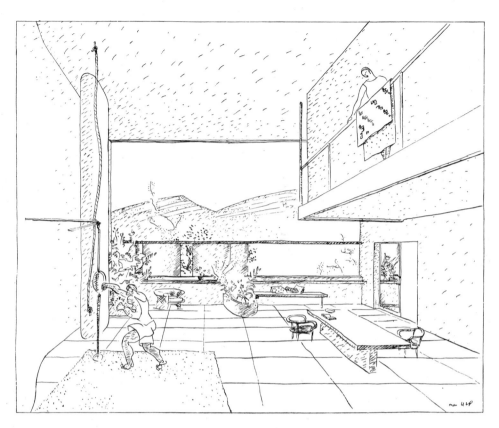

25. Terrace Garden, Geneva, 1928, perspective. Le Corbusier.

Le Corbusier: Utopian Architect

planning proposals was severely criticized by all participants. In addition, a general feeling was expressed that the period of his greatest influence on contemporaries was already drawing to an end. Although it was suggested by Berthold Lubetkin that Le Corbusier had never been Utopian enough and had concerned himself too exclusively with expedients, this was not the general view. Graeme Shankland felt that Le Corbusier's tendency to make man in his own image, to project this image on society and often to impose a formal pattern regardless of circumstances, in some degree vitiated his contribution. James Stirling expressed the opinion that the spatial luxury which was necessary to all his achievement was now beginning to detract from the viability of his forms, and proposed that in the post-Corbusier world a more down-to-earth empiricism was to be desired. Both George Kassaboff and I myself registered a mild disagreement with this view. If Le Corbusier's Utopianism does seem to have been such a powerful agent of change in the 1920s and 1930s, is it not also reasonable to suppose that if change is required, then another Utopian attitude might well again provide the stimulus?

But how quickly I changed my mind about Utopia . . .

The Blenheim of the Welfare State

Published in *The Cambridge Review,* October, 31, 1959

On the whole I think that this was, and is, a significant piece of empirical criticism and that it may have exercised some influence on the final form of the buildings at Churchill College. But, surely, I was too hopeful in suggesting that the Stirling and Gowan solution would be extensively imitated since their parti seems to have been entirely without any issue. It derives from, or so I think, a little village in southern Mexico, Chiapas de Corzo, which I once described to Jim.

A work of architecture is invariably an advertisement of a point of view. It is never either pure form or pure function; nor can it simply be a mixture of both; but always it involves an act of judgement. It is an attitude taken up with regard to society, history, change, the nature of pleasure, and other matters quite extraneous to either technique or taste. Thus, a work of architecture, while always an index to state of mind, may quite often be construed as an illicit manifesto; and the typical work of Modern architecture was, until recently, quite often to be interpreted in this way. Thinly disguised, it was a polemic about modernity; and for that reason it was apt to involve all our sentiments about science and mechanization, the good society, the necessity of planning, the idea of progress, and the inexorable *Zeitgeist*. Allegedly the building was innocent of all these overtones, but they were for all that a poetic medium which was the cause of half its appeal. Explicitly the building was a product of an empirical common sense and a scientific handling of problems. But implicitly it pointed a moral. A criticism of custom, an assault upon the status quo, an exhortation to reform, it was put forward as an exemplary fragment of future order which had been interjected into present chaos.

But the future has an inconvenient way of catching up with the present, so that a radical movement can easily lose focus and a polemical attitude can often come to appear superfluous; and if in this predicament we recognize the typical and recurrent debacle of the left, we might notice that this is just as much the architectural reality of the present day as it is the political one. Disraeli "caught the Whigs bathing and stole their clothes"; and something of the same kind has happened in the recent history of architecture, with the result that the symbolic trophies of an epoch of reform are now paraded by all parties alike. It is an ironical situation. To some it is embarrassing. But it is a situation always to be expected; and one which, appropriately enough, forms the general setting for the Churchill College competition.

The didactic orientation of Modern architecture then has become somewhat attenuated and confused; and no doubt this could explain the labyrinthine quality of certain of the contributions and the rather disappointing nature of the ultimate judgement; but this condition, endemic to architecture at the moment, is perhaps only a very minor component of an analysis of Churchill; and any adequate analysis requires a recognition of at least three levels of difficulty with which the competitors were obliged to contend.

At a purely factual level, on a not very interesting site alongside the Madingley Road a number of rooms of varying sizes and uses were to be disposed with some regard to convenience and some regard to order. At a more referential level, these rooms were to accommodate and denote a college; and finally this college, a society animated by a common mystique, dedicated primarily to scientific pursuits, implicated with the name of a great and volatile Conservative statesman, was to stand in certain functional and symbolic relationships with the university, the country, and the world.

These problems are arranged in ascending order of complexity but are obviously interrelated at all points. Precisely how the site on Madingley Road was to be exploited, how its suburban monotony was to be dispelled, how it was to be equipped with an artificial *genius loci*—all this quite clearly depended on how a college was to be denoted, how a common mystique was to be implied, whether an archetypal college could be deduced or whether a quintessence of the peculiar virtues of a Cambridge college could be distilled; and these questions in themselves became inextricably involved, and perhaps controlled, by the reasonable assumption that the buildings of a Churchill college should be in some way be Churchillian—buildings perhaps big in scale, exuberant, simple, pugnacious, uncompromising, and, to a degree, rhetorical.

The average naive individual construes, and perhaps he somehow misconstrues, much of what has been left unsaid; but somehow he acquires the impression that Churchill College, a training ground for a scientific elite, is also in some sense a monument. He intuits perhaps that a collegiate body is not a person and that a building cannot be a portrait; but, for all that, he anticipates that, as a home for this new institution, he will discover a statement of symbolic consequence. Dimly he conceives a structure which will induce some feeling of *pietas.* More dimly he imagines a building which will condense into a single image the recollection of an heroic past and the anticipation of an effulgent future.

But to be practical: if this is what the average naive individual expects, it is difficult to see how it could have been done. No

The Blenheim of the Welfare State

doubt it was *the* idea. Certainly it *ought* to have been done. Several competitors have felt the necessity of attempting it. But to have done it with success would have required an architect of Churchillian eloquence and experience, and after the restrictions on building in the last years there are no such figures to be found. In a number of schemes, it is true, the theme of monument is conceded—by the appearance of a rather corpulent figure, usually labelled 'Statue of Founder.' One feels that these sculptural exercises would scarcely be edifying and would probably be painful, and one suspects that it is only when the monumental intention reaches a more idealized plane that it becomes in any way moving. The huge obelisk with which Sir Hugh Casson and Neville Conder furnish their project (a recollection of, presumably, Washington, D.C.) is apparently the only instance of an idealized "monument as such"; and interestingly enough, the deference which Casson and his partner pay to the retrospective aspects of the programme has provided them with a most valuable opportunism for the development of the terrain. The Casson obelisk is so enormous and could so easily verge on the sublime that one most seriously regrets that it will never be built. It would have provided a centre of gravity in the western part of Cambridge. It would have entered into the profile of the town along with King's Chapel, the Library, the Church of the English Martyrs, and miscellaneous industrial buildings. It would have located the college and particularized the site; and though it would have been despised by purists, infallibly it would have become a part of the idea of the university.

The scheme by Stirling and Gowan, which introduces the adjective *Churchillian* with rather more abstracted connotations— by presenting the spectacle of an intransigent and very memorable building—conveniently leads from the problem of monument to the problem of collegiate form in general. On the whole there has been remarkable unanimity of opinion as to what a college should be. It seems to have been agreed that a college implies a courtyard and that the more courtyards a college possesses, the more collegiate it is likely to become. Thus there has been in this competition what

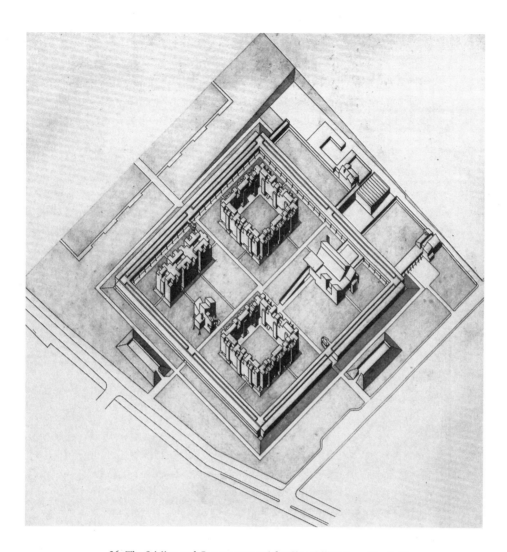

26. The Stirling and Gowan proposal for Churchill College, Cambridge.

The Blenheim of the Welfare State

one is tempted to describe as an epidemic of claustrophilia; and, once infected by it, most competitors seem to have been satisfied to take any number of courts, to press them into either complicated or casual relationship, to flavour them all with an aroma of Cambridge (understood to be a demure charm), and to complete the whole with reminiscences or Le Corbusier or Scandinavia. Only Alison and Peter Smithson have remained aloof from this claustrophile enthusiasm and have produced an outward looking building which might quite well be an appropriate image for a scientific institution.

But allowing that a college almost certainly should require a courtyard; and that this is a matter which, like the monumental issue, *ought* to be solved, Stirling and Gowan have perhaps come closer to a viable organization for colleges in general than any other competitors. They have rejected the assumption that a college is simply a benign and womb-like atmosphere and have insisted that its form should correspond to some disposition which the mind can immediately digest. They have, perhaps somewhat obsessively, insisted that this means one courtyard and one courtyard only; but having done so they have provided a solution which, as a thesis, is impeccable.

The great problem of the college courtyard, when judged by other than picturesque criteria, is the intrusion into the enclosing wall surface of a variety of large elements—chapels, dining halls, libraries—which are exceptionally difficult to bring into any relationship with the student sets which provide the basic unit of scale. Stirling and his partner present an exceptionally direct approach to this problem. In principle they discriminate between an enclosing wall of student rooms and, distributed within the space which is thus framed, a series of independent pavilions serving communal functions. The proposition is lucid and entirely convincing; but unfortunately this ideal classification has not received from its originators all the respect which it seems to deserve and they have, to some extent, violated their own hierarchy of significance by introducing, within the courtyard, elements of the same functional value as those which they have used to enclose it.

But in spite of this unfortunate confusion of categories, the Stirling and Gowan scheme, as the courtyard gambit in the abstract, provides a model which *does* deserve to be intensively studied and which *will* be extensively imitated. Their building is as detached, as aloof from the Cambridge idea as the Gibbs Building. Like Gibbs it aspires to universality, and its unflinching exterior allows it to tell in an entirely insulated position. This is surely important, since the Cambridge college, buttressed by and interwoven with the fabric of the town, is for the most part always an interior. It never requires to present a continuous exterior to the world. It protrudes parts, exhibits a screen or a gate, confronts a landscape with a loggia; but it always avoids the difficulties of a complete, consistent, in the round suite of facades. In Churchill College this can scarcely be the case. The building stands free; and the problem presented is therefore infinitely more elaborate. As in the case of the Gibbs building and the Palladian house in the English park, there is a great deal to be said for a stiffening of the exterior so as to provide a definite volumetric field which will prevent all edges and definition becoming blurred. At least this is classical practice; and it is only to be expected that Stirling and Gowan, who seem to aspire to what Dr. Johnson called "the grandeur of generality," should have adopted it. However, the archetypal college which haunted the imagination of these two was not exactly a popular theme among the mass of the competitors; and the entirely opposite theme, the college which is unique rather than exemplary, was stated with superlative conviction by Howell, Killick, and Partridge, who, since they responded to the particular conditions of the location more than any other competitors, will here prompt a digression into this last range of difficulties.

There was a problem in the Churchill programme, not stated but very easily felt: that of inducing an illusion that Madingley Road somehow subserves the college buildings and only seriously leads off to St. Neots when it has left them behind, a problem of articulating the length of Madingley Road. And there was a further problem: that Madingley Road and Storey's Way both alike require recognition. As an artery linking the site with Cambridge, the first is obviously the more important of the two, and the mind seems to require that the buildings should make some decisive gesture towards it. On the other hand, as a means of sorting out possible traffic confusion, an entrance on Storey's Way presents itself as an imperative.

This conflict of interests is one to which a number of competitors have been sensitive. Chamberlin, Powell, and Bon have inflated Storey's Way to the prominence of a piazza. The Smithsons have inflected their H-shaped group of towers towards the intersection of the two roads. Fry, Drew, Drake, and Lasdun have done something of the same kind. Casson and Conder have stabilized this corner area of the site by allowing an entrance for pedestrians from Madingley Road and an entrance for automobiles and bicycles from Storey's Way. A first virtue of the Howell, Killick, and Partridge scheme is to have pressed this interpretation a stage further. They have dragged Casson and Conder's somewhat recessive entrance forward into a position of prominence, so that it punctuates the Madingley Road, penetrates the site at its most crucial point, gives precedence to the pedestrian, and still permits the traffic entrance from Storey's Way.

Once this is recognized, like all other clear solutions, it becomes perfectly obvious, elementary, and natural; and there would be nothing more to be said if this Howell contribution did not in all parts display the same cool and professional attention to problems which its entrance arrangements demonstrate. But the major elements of this scheme are all beautifully articulated. It has, as the assessors recognized, a complete consistency, inner and outer. It is rich, intricate, and beautifully simple; and where Stirling's scheme would control an environment by force of contour, this building, animated by an inner turbulence, would project an environment in almost musical fashion.

After either of these two designs (and several others) it is not agreeable to approach the winning one, and no critics appear to have found it easy to do so. It is an adequate building. It has many merits. It may well make a good college. It is almost certainly better than might have been expected if no competition had been organised. But it is no plastic exhortation. Neat, tidy, bland, well-intentioned, and cautious, for all its virtues this Blenheim of the welfare state induces a wriggle of embarrassment, arouses a yawn of anticlimax, and (in some quarters) has encouraged a smile of derision. One sympathizes with the assessors. Their choice, which must have been scrupulous, could not have been easy. Nowhere but in England and at no time in England but the mid-twentieth century could a sublime idea have been quashed by so incongruous an evocation.

The Blenheim of the Welfare State

A Vote of Thanks

I believe that the occasion arose at the Architectural Association in the late spring of 1959 and, no doubt, this piece is to be found in the AA Journal *of about that date. Of course I never should have consented to give any vote of thanks in Bedford Square, and certainly I should have had ready a bland little something to say. But the full pitch of self-righteous anti-American innuendo to which I was compelled to listen was, on the whole, slightly excoriating.*

In proposing a vote of thanks to Mr. Medd I find it somewhat disconcerting to begin because I do not know quite what to say. However, if I begin by confessing this dilemma, it is possible that I might solve it by some means or other—although quite how I do not know.

I have always been horrified by arguments from experience; and in my case—if I may give you my experience—I have spent some seven years in the United States. However, I do not feel that it is experience that counts but rather the state of mind which is directed to coordinate experience.

Now, the speaker and I seem to share so many sympathies in common but seem to be divided at certain stages by misunderstandings so acute that I am not quite sure how I should thank him. But I do want to thank him for stimulating and also for arousing me. It is a little hard to thank him and also to disagree with him because quite evidently the angels are on his side; and because I enjoyed so many things which aroused his indignation, and because in some cases—but not many—I have been indignant at things about which he has enthused, I am left with the feeling that I must be on the side of the devil.

Going off on a tangent for a moment, possibly to build up a point of view: during a considerable length of time in America I never heard a particular vocabulary which I hear in England, consisting of such words as *hip, square, cool,* etc. There are other words that go with these but I never heard any of them until they came over in architectural magazines from England. I asked the people around me what these words meant. They said that they were not sure but they believed that they were something to do with jazz terminology and possibly used by juvenile delinquents in certain metropolitan centres. They were surprised that they were being used in England. A sense of decorum was offended by the idea. However, what does the use of these words represent? Why does the English intelligentsia apparently enjoy using these words—*cool, square, dig,* etc.? If you like they are a form of semantic costume jewellery with which one strews one's speech. But why does one do it? What effect does one get from their use? I suppose they make you sound truthful. They make you sound as though you have a grip on reality. They make you sound sympathetic and democratic. They probably even have some implication of sexual potency. They imply somehow a picture of a noble savage in a state of nature who uses this vocabulary as a matter of course. The Europeans do have this point of view with regard to the Americans, and this often accounts for their disappointments. If you expect a noble savage living in Eden—even if it is only an American Eden—and if you find out he is not so noble or not so savage as you hoped he was going to be, it is rather disappointing. It is also, I suppose, disappointing that, while England is soft and blurred and rather pretty, America is hard, distinct, and often quite ugly. The effect of America is often like having the sensitive parts of one's body rubbed over with sandpaper of a rather coarse description, and the effect of England is never this—until one has been quite a long time out of the country, when it is identically abrasive.

But I have got the impression from the speech that everything in England must be OK; that somehow God has revealed himself at some stage of history to the London County Council; that a new heaven and a new earth are about to begin. This is quite literally the picture that I have received. It does not jell with my experience. I wish it did. But I cannot see that it does.

Obviously vulgarity, or something like it, will always be with us. It is never going to be expunged. Architects can become as Christ-like as ever they wish and be prepared to sacrifice themselves for a new Jerusalem around the corner. But this new Jerusalem is not going to drive vulgarity out of the world. It will only bring it back in a new disguise. Really Modern architecture has only resulted in new disguises for new vulgarity. Not much more than that. And it is where this process has been quicker than it has in England that the vulgarity appears to be more acute. One has been subjected to certain fantasies about how wonderful Modern architecture is, and then one suddenly sees quite a lot of things which tell a different story—ice cream parlours or places for drinking orange juice strewn along the roadside, all 'modern'—and merely by repetition the thing is vulgarised. This stage of repetition has not arrived here as yet, although devaluation is pretty far gone in some ways. You can skim through the pictures in *House and Garden,* and, looking at so-called Modern buildings, you can begin to wonder if the situation is so very different here from that in the United States. But there are some explanations which one has to drag in to provide

A Vote of Thanks

some understanding of American architecture; and I was struck the other day in Corb's *Towards a New Architecture* by the last chapter, entitled "Architecture or Revolution." You are left with these two things and the question: Which is it going to be? Maybe if you select architecture you will frustrate revolution, or if you select architecture you will encourage revolution. You are never quite sure. But the possibilities of either or both excite you.

I do not think that you can play this theme to American architects or to American audiences. Chiefly, I think, because when they think of revolutions or *the revolution,* they think of something which took place in 1776. Their mood is entirely retrospective. The idea of a prospective revolutionary event simply does not enter the picture. That I think would be the chief difference in state of mind between the English or European and the American architect. I would suspect that the European architect is often preoccupied with an image of the Middle Ages. He tries to put it away from him and therefore imagines a revolution as something which is going to free society and introduce a new and just order represented by buildings. In America it does not work that way—but I seem to be giving another lecture when I should in any case be proposing a vote of thanks.

While thanking the speaker I would suspect that running through his address there are two assumptions. One, stated with considerable reservation, is that America is rather a bad thing, except when there are cases of extreme collectivism; when the second assumption comes into play and it becomes rather a good thing. Now, although I am sure that we would react in almost the same way to many physical manifestations we might meet, this would separate us; and this enables me to qualify my vote of thanks because I would put matters the other way around. I feel collectivism to be rather a bad thing, and I prefer America when it is least collectivistic. In other words, I should not get really wildly excited about children playing about on the periphery of a shopping centre and all that.

157

However, I have listened with considerable instruction.
Having spent quite a long time on such frontiers of the Western
world as Texas, I have tended to think that possibly in the metro-
polises of the Western world the level of, shall we say, performance,
was higher than one actually discovers it to be. And this is quite
gratifying because it encourages one to think that, in spite of vulgar-
ities, maybe places like Texas and California are really in the right.
They are probably not gratifying places. But driving around this
country I see little to gratify *me.* Having driven from Texas to New
York and back again and having driven at Easter into Wales and
back again, I am left wondering on what ground we can base any
criticism at all. I looked at Gloucester cathedral on the way. I was
depressed by this Gothic junk heap. I looked at Hereford. It was
rather worse. On the way back I came through Shrewsbury. I arrived at eight o'clock. It was impossible to have dinner. *Too* late!
And so at six-thirty the following morning I got up, and from then
until about eight-thirty I walked around Shrewsbury and discovered on my walk two rather bad, rather dirty, rather scruffy, red
sandstone Gothic churches, a number of black and white houses of
remarkably little merit, rather sub-peasant in quality, and a dull re-
siduum of late eighteenth century opulence. And this was Shrewsbury. And the only evidence that mind had ever existed was a
statue, a rather inept one, commemorating the birth of Charles
Darwin.

This is the experience which a more or less dispassionate observer might gain in driving around England, without a good deal
of the physical elation which might be experienced, which I know
the speaker has experienced, in driving around the United States.
Therefore, although I have enjoyed listening, I would have been hap-
pier if I had felt that the speaker had not tried to inhibit his natural
and immediate reaction to things and to moralise a situation which
he discovered to be embarrassing.

A Vote of Thanks

Review: Student Work of the Architectural Association

Published in the *AA Journal*, 1959

This piece could be helped by better illustrations of the student work of that period; but apart from that, it requires no explanation. I think, though, that it might have led to Tony Eardley's coming to Cambridge in the following year—at the same time as Jacquelin Robertson and Peter Eisenman.

The AA manner of the moment is a little like an outburst of Pont Street Dutch after a wave of Belgravian stucco. Capable for these reasons of immediately fitting into the London scene and of augmenting its variety, it is therefore a paradoxical style which betrays a preference for the particular rather than the general, for the striking rather than the exemplary. In some ways a deliberate sabotage of the older Modern architecture, in others a rather hectic loyalty towards it, at the level of forms it apparently consists of multiple reminiscences. Thus the dry bones of the Ville Radieuse are ruthlessly agitated, and the Unité at Marseilles is violently hacked about; the once discredited expressionists of the 1920s are again pressed into service; Constructivism and De Stijl are allowed to provide significant ingredients; the contributions of Art Nouveau and Futurism are not neglected; and then, with an affectation of deliberate casualness, the whole amalgam is savagely stirred to be ultimately moulded with a regard for its potential *terribilità*.

These are not adverse comments. States of mind can be explained. Most of these ingredients do come from the very best purveyors; and, if there is something a little obsessive about the process of putting them together, there is also a welcome authenticity about the result. These projects for buildings are never unpleasantly ingratiating. They are not sugary. They are not inflated. They are rarely whimsical and never coy. Nor are they provincial. They are for the most part honest. They are generally self-conscious. They usually betray the evidence of conviction. The observer does not feel that he is being tricked, does not feel that his judgement is being subverted. But on the other hand the observer need not feel exactly exhilarated. And to say why requires some examination of this exhibition at the level of forms and functions and then, perhaps, some further examination at the level of attitudes involved. Stylistically, except for certain aberrant contributions, most of the schemes exhibited fall into two groups. There is a series of buildings rather like enlarged pieces of mechanical furniture or elaborate and variously opened chests of drawers; and there is another series of more biomorphic intent, in extreme cases slightly intestinal in their implications and apt to sprout a variety of tubes and similar extrusions. This second group is more than apt to be comprised of concert halls and miscellaneous auditoria; while the first group is more strictly reserved for residential or possibly commercial purposes. It is possible that both groups may give offence to the conservatively minded; but then, since it is obvious that they are intended to do so, we must consider them to be successful in at least one specific aim.

For myself, I am sympathetic to the first group and experience a certain antipathy towards the second. But these are matters of personal preference and judgement and one should, if possible, not concern oneself simply with questions of taste. At one level, at the level of forms and functions, architecture consists in the assigning of pattern to space and matter; and at this level it may very well be claimed that the critic can make no valid objection to any type of pattern which is assigned but that he can only object if pattern is inconsistent with itself or does violence to the object in which it is embodied. And a first question therefore might be whether we are made aware of any such inconsistencies or acts of violence. But, if this is so, in rather too many cases, I think, it is necessary to answer this question with an affirmative.

The cult of extreme plasticity does after all have certain important consequences; and it is here, when we imagine ourselves inside certain projects which are on the face of it so stimulating, that we are apt to be made a little uncomfortable. High articulation of elevation is quite often unaccompanied by any corresponding high articulation of plan and section. Explosive juxtapositions of volume are quite frequently not explained by any inner turbulence. The outdoor and indoor games, which are really one and the same, are apt to be played according to quite different rules. Of the two, the outdoor game is likely to be the more enterprising. Thus plans suffer, are apt to be a little trite, insufficiently correlated with plastic expression. As a result, space is only too rarely something which is firm, stratified, and substantial, a something which can almost be touched. In other cases too where such inconsistencies cannot be attributed, where the exterior is infallibly a projection of an interior, as in the various concert halls and cinemas which are displayed, one is again quite often made aware of inadequacy of solution, although here, since there is rather too general a tendency to allow motif to take control at the expense of function, it is with acts of violence that we are concerned.

Thus there are, and one should not have to say it, certain building species where function is so explicit or can so readily be discriminated that it must inevitably dictate form; and these species of building may be compared to types of utensil in which shape is necessarily appropriate to services performed. These are species of building in which, in terms of function, it is possible to envisage an ideal solution—almost in the same way that we can assert the form of a sieve, or a funnel, or a spray, or a teapot to be ideal. Now, like many simple utensils such as these, an auditorium is inherently of a symmetrical nature; and deviation from this basic banality is really only to be justified if it can be explained as being conditioned by particular exigencies. Given such exigencies, a battle can break out between the conceptually 'correct' auditorium of the mind and the implacably 'real' circumstances of the occasion; tensions can be established; a rigorous dialectic can ensue between what *should* be and what *has* to be; displacements can result; and all this will be acceptable and even stimulating because distortion of the building's 'natural' shape can be accounted for by reason of some peculiar local difficulty. But if the observer cannot explain distortion by reasons such as these, as in several cases in this exhibition he cannot, then inevitably he finds himself in the presence of what he believes to be an arbitrary phenomenon. Plastically the object he experiences may be exciting but intellectually it cannot be inordinately convincing.

It is scarcely possible in a brief review of this kind to particularise criticism more than this; but obviously certain schemes do rise above these general remarks or in any case continue to impress in spite of their failings. Thus, from the third year, there are two projects, a home for maladjusted children and a museum, both by Bernard Knight, which are beautifully constructed, assertive without exaggeration, and which, for me, are the two most entirely convincing contributions to this exhibition.

From the year below a small and somewhat expressionist house by Simon Sprent leaves me almost equally impressed; and though perhaps a little underscaled in its spaces, the achievement which it represents is made very clear when it is compared with the admirable houses by M. L. Haxworth and David Dixon, alongside which it is displayed. Perhaps no fourth year auditorium is equal to

Edward Reynold's building of two years ago; but although one may
be exasperated in some cases by extravagance of section and in others by devious entrance arrangements and painful seating conditions, one is still made aware that, for instance, Timothy Tinker's
cinema or Nabil Tabbara's concert hall are not achievements which
can be overlooked. Possibly the fourth year was a little too much at
a loss in its replanning of Westminster, too committed to a Futurist
aesthetic and too frightened of the apparatus of the baroque city
to create any really memorable specimen of urban order; but for
all that, proposals for Westminster do include a good many ideas
which persist in the mind, among them the castle complex by Boot,
Tinker, and Thompson ought surely to be noticed. But in addition
to these few selected pieces there is a good deal else in which one
recognises a level of quality: in the first year the houses by West-
mann and Johnson; in the second year the petrol stations by Har-
rison and Hirshmann; in the third year the museum by Lynn; in the
fourth the kasbah by Matthew, Stone, Summers, and Tabbara: and
also in the fourth year those strange quasi-Mackintoshian, quasi–
Gothic Revival exercises through which a group of apparently anonymous students attempt to express a position of extreme dissent.

These last are certainly the most surprising exhibits in the
whole show, and the note of interrogation they strike might provide
a convenient opportunity of bringing to an end this rather tedious
catalogue of the virtues (which threatens to become rather like a dis-
tribution of prizes) and of directing attention towards the drift, or
the tendency, or the will which this exhibition represents.

By way of diagnosis of this will or trend a quotation might
be allowed: "It is," says Santayana, "in the nature of the pioneer that
the greater his success the quicker must be his transformation into
something different"; and, if there is a degree of truth in this, one
might also recognise that it corresponds to recent experience. Characteristically the Modern architect has conceived himself to be a pioneer, and lately inevitable fate has caught up with him.

It is now some years since Modern architecture began to
turn into 'something different', to turn into a popular success; and

Student Work of the Architectural Association

it is some years since the perceptive began to recognise that this process had certainly devalued the complex imagery by which the
movement had originally been animated. For the figure of the architect as a pioneer on the frontiers of the future became increasingly
irrelevant as the anticipated future became increasingly imminent;
while the anticipated future itself became curiously divested of ideal
overtones as its attainment became more and more of a possibility.
Thus the long awaited recognition of Modern architecture has
turned out to be something of an anticlimax. The architect has, to
an extent, superseded his own conception of himself. But to approach the problem with somewhat more highly coloured criteria:
twenty years ago, or perhaps even ten, if one had been asked to provide allegorical representation of the then new architect, one might
have done far worse than select the figure of David, or the ingenuous and youthful innovator confronting the great and stupid Philistine. But one could scarcely do this today. Times change. The stone
hits the mark. Goliath falls. The historic David pays the penalty for
his audaciousness. Converted into a legend, limited by the precedent he has established, condemned to routine, he becomes perhaps
something of a Philistine himself—and in any case his performance
provides the model for subsequent Philistine generations, so that
those who seek to inherit his role are often confounded by the ef-
forts of those who have already preempted it. This classic post-
revolutionary predicament can be framed in any number of ways,
but here these two very imperfect cross sections must suffice to illustrate its nature; while the nature of the predicament itself must also
suffice as explanation of the present and immediately preceding exhi-
bitions at the AA. For desperate situations often require desperate
measures; and, without any excess of critical generosity, these exhibi-
tions can be attributed to a disgust with over-acceptable formulae;
and they can also be justified as attempting to give back to Modern
architecture a significance which it has lost.

But though one respects the motivating idea and admires
some of its results, one need not altogether agree as to the means. It
is a characteristic of shock treatment that the more it is applied, the

less efficacious it is likely to be. It is a spiral: the patient becomes insensitive to the prescribed stimuli, he demands more frequent shocks of greater violence, and then he becomes insensitive again; and one might recognise that the present exhibition, by comparison with the salutary shock of 1957, has failed.

To pass further judgement is possible only at the risk of sententiousness and also at the risk of standing on a very shaky critical base. The observer may wish to stigmatise the AA exhibition as dissenting, schismatic, and heretical; but in order to do so he has to say from what it dissents. He is placed therefore in the ambiguous position of affirming the significance of one revolution and of refusing to attribute value to a further movement of reform. In fact he is placed a little in the position of a member of the eighteenth century Anglican establishment, pronouncing the Reformation to have been a return to the primitive virtues and therefore a good thing but condemning, say, the Methodists as dangerous enthusiasts. And is this very consistent? Or is it very defensible? Obviously it is neither. It is a deplorable position. But for all that it may sometimes be a position which we ought to accept.

Student Work of the Architectural Association

Review: *A Testament* by Frank Lloyd Wright

Returning to England in 1958 to teach at Cambridge, obviously I must have felt some compulsion to communicate recent experience; and, as a result, for a time I was—by my standards—pretty prolific. This review of Frank Lloyd Wright's last book, **A Testament,** *is a product of that period. It was proposed by Leonie Cohn, who had something to do with the talks department at the BBC, and when I submitted this review, it evidently met with less than approval. And I can understand why. It was altogether too elaborate for the occasion. Nevertheless, because—as they say in Italy—it is* suggestivo *and because I don't want it to become wholly lost, I have thought it permissible to present the piece as originally written here. Though written in England it is intimately relatable to my recent Texas experience; and, needless to say, it remains incomplete.*

168

In a famous passage Matthew Arnold speaks of "the Celts, with their vehement reaction against the despotism of fact, with their sensuous nature, their manifold striving, their adverse destiny, their immense calamities." It provides a useful opening gambit. It is the type of cultural summary, very rhetorical and large, which Frank Lloyd Wright might well have appreciated. For it was surely in these terms that he thought of himself; and, if the type of ethnic discrimination which Arnold practiced so well is no longer in fashion, one can still feel that a prophetic specification was here provided by him, both of Wright's genius and his career. For obviously it is not only as a trans-Atlantic phenomenon that Wright must be envisaged. Like his near contemporary, David Lloyd George, he remained aboriginally Welsh; and that eminently Cymric strain, with its sentimentalism and its sensibility, its perceptiveness, turbulence, spontaneity, indiscipline, and above all its moral and intellectual enthusiasm—that strain which in the United Kingdom is so often frustrated—must in Wright be seen first as emancipated by an American milieu and, second, as struggling with the social order that made it free. For that Welsh passion for words and *the word,* that tendency to declamation, that propensity to preach—while it found in American Puritanism a congenial soil, while it allied itself to the mid-nineteenth century Massachusetts respect for the revelations of German philosophy, while it appreciated and revered rationalist America—was always at war with that greatest and most famous monument to the Enlightenment which is the United States.

Alike in the wilds of Merioneth and in the highlands of Tennessee, in the vicinity of Aberystwyth or Dolgelly, around Nashville or Chattanooga, Wright, with less education than he had received, would not have been without notoriety as a fundamentalist preacher. He had the temperament. He could assume the role. But, if one may imagine him unconcerned with plastic ideas, in late Victorian Wales, as a bardic figure progressively drawn into politics, acquiring first a seat at Westminster and, second, a controversial reputation, if in the United Kingdom it might have been as a representative of the Rhondda that he would win recognition, in the United States the simplicities of public life were not in any way able to claim him. By the obligations of place, he was a Welshman condemned to private sophistication; and though he retained, like Lloyd George, that taste for the apparatus of personality—sticks, hats, cloak, hair—though lonely against the stormy backdrop, his was the same instinct for self-dramatisation, with him the imbuing histrionic energy of the race was compelled to service another range of phantasy. He had been exposed—however vicariously—to the Alexandrine urbanities of Transcendentalist Boston. The message of Emerson had come his way. Charles Eliot Norton had not proclaimed his devotion to Ruskin without effect. And all these ideas, translated with the family on their return to rural Wisconsin, were to issue entangled with more purely indigenous American myth: the Jeffersonian ideal of the agrarian community and the Whitmanesque exaltation of the pioneer.

As a way of bringing him into focus, one may pause to think of Wright and of the present appearance of the world had his father remained a Unitarian minister in Boston—perhaps attending the Roxbury Latin School with George Santayana, almost certainly at Harvard a student of William James and a classmate not only of Bernard Berenson but of Logan Pearsall Smith. But if the strain on the imagination is too great, by following the example of Lionel Brett one can still frame Wright's achievement in a comparison between him and Edwin Lutyens. Wright dissimulated his age. Born in 1867, he wished to have been born in 1869; and in this year of course the nativity of his English contemporary did take place. Both were gifted. Both from careful backgrounds. Both inherited certain traditions in common. And though they were separated by the spiritual gulf which intervenes between Surrey and Wisconsin, for a time at least their performances ran in parallel.

But there were distinctions. In America there are no Blenheims. The program of the great country house has never magnetised the architecture of the United States. It was never a socially viable idea. In an egalitarian society it would have been considered

Review: *A Testament*

an offensive manifestation. And accordingly, at a comparatively early date the problem of the medium-sized residence, attracting towards itself not only competence but talent, was able to result in a quantity of solutions of a strictness of plan and polish elsewhere not attainable. The English late eighteenth century had seen the rise of that most popular of bourgeois forms: the picturesque detached house. In England it was obliged to jostle for position, but as item of cultural export, in America it was provided with an empty theatre for display. In England, brutalised by the polemic of the Gothic Revival or made precious by the followers of Norman Shaw, it progressively languished in suburban squalor to become an object of neo-Georgian contempt. But in America, where it was everything and all, fused with an unsurpassed tradition of small scale domestic refinement, transposed from stucco to timber, retaining its Regency vivacity, increasingly invested with a bravura, it was enabled to issue as perhaps the most significant contribution to the architecture of the last two hundred years. It was this tradition, not esoteric, central to society, the preferred taste of an extensive, an opulent, and a cultivated middle class, that Wright inherited.

Lutyens was in no such enviable position. For the same tradition as received by him had never been appropriated to itself by more than a narrow sector of society; and though it had been revitalised by the neo-Picturesque of the Queen Anne Revival, refurbished with sparkle and with brilliant textural effects, it had not like its American counterpart received a specific animation which only Paris could contribute. The English plan remained compartmentalised. In spite of Regency attempts to make internal configuration of space respond to the contours of the exterior, the English medium-sized residence, for all its virtues, had persisted very largely as an inert piece of scenery. Often exceedingly well executed and detailed with solicitous enthusiasm, the English small house, for all its virtues, still made it abundantly clear that its architects had scarcely struggled to arrive at any rationale of their activity. They had received the dispensation of a Norman Shaw, but the dispensation of a Richardson was beyond their knowledge. And Richardson held all the cards. American by birth, English by sympathy, French by training, Richardson in his short career towers above all possible rivals. By his side Norman Shaw becomes a clever watercolourist. Richardson reduces the splendidly endowed Charles Garnier to the status of a meretricious decorator. And it was the inheritance of a French rationalism, transmitted through him by the Laboustes, which, above all else, permitted the sudden conversion of the Picturesque house from a popular formula into a spatial explosion. Richardson introduced logic. He had acquired the Parisian rigor; he had compounded it with the passion of a Butterfield; and he had made it operative via his most personal ability, both to control the profile of the local episode and to soften the edge of the total mass. With him the cultivation of the arbitrary seemed always to be propelled by internal necessity; the whimsies so dear to the nineteenth century always to be proliferated by principle; and the plan to become something like the music of an opera of which the integrated libretto comprised the details.

This brilliant synthesis of the English and the French, eliminating the weaknesses of both, recalling something of the American political synthesis of a century earlier, was unique to North America. Europe at that date had nothing to show of comparable eminence. After the death of the equally Paris-directed Cockerell, England could offer no such superb example of professionalism; and Lutyens, without any equivalent reservoir of accomplishment on which to draw, was constrained to exploit his congenital feeling for improvisation and all the national sympathy for the amateur.

Thus, although Lutyens and Wright for a brief period were superficially close, it was only a matter of time before the great cleavage began to appear.

Wright—the *anima naturaliter classica,* to borrow from Henry-Russell Hitchcock—had already by the nineties in his designs for the Milwaukee Public Library and the Blossom House, Chicago, anticipated those classicizing tendencies which were later to provide the English architect with his stock in trade. American prescience and Celtic quickness had forced to the surface and had overcome certain issues.

Review: *A Testament*

In addition Wright married no Lady Emily Lytton. He inherited by proxy no viceregal splendours. No effulgence like that of the raj was enabled to divert his course. No British Knebworth lay, like an instructive shadow, across his career. For Americans of his generation and attainments, a move into public life was far from easy; and the sense of exclusion from political society which had already nurtured a Henry Adams seems in Wright's generation to have contributed a peculiar brilliancy to intellectual life. The possibility of identifying with government, never hard for an Englishman and facilitated for Lutyens by his connections, issued in England as approximate determinations of form, as empirical working procedures. But the impossibility of identifying with government seems to have sponsored in the United States a vein of introspection and an aesthetic culture which could never be satisfied with less than a final statement. And thus while the English architect, as he achieves prominence, can become more and more like the mouthpiece of government, more and more like the mannered representative of the English system in all its supposedly august presence, these are potentialities or privileges of which the American is largely deprived. And in the case of Lutyens and Wright, we are finally awarded the ironical commentary of Lutyens in England painfully suppressing his bohemianism, becoming the agent of an exclusive dream of imperium, while his wife—more certain of her position—cultivates her taste for Krishnamurti and other theosophical manifestations; and of Wright in America, strenuously maintaining a personal rebellion, assuming both Lady Emily's interest in Orientalia *and* her husband's architectural activity, going out to meet the most varied experience with nothing to uphold but principle. And, taken side by side, the Imperial Hotel, Tokyo, and the Viceroy's House, New Delhi, complete the illumination of the point.

But before proceeding to the review of the book of which this article is the ostensible pretext, one more odious comparison may still be helpful. English intellectual traditions often incline toward the Continent. To whatever emanates from that source there is

sometimes a tendency to attribute intellect. That anything should
come from elsewhere may on occasion appear an intolerable scandal.
And let us therefore put Wright into further perspective, not by
measuring him against Le Corbusier but by using the one to qualify
the other. The great French system maker and the great American
chameleon: we are presented with two species of dissent, two alternative moral codes, ultimately with the rival orthodoxies of Rome
and Geneva. And on the side of Rome, for all his near-Geneva background, we will place Le Corbusier. His is the symmetrical intellect
which seeks to abstract experience into a single harmonious vision—into one inexorable, consistent, lucid, controlling, and all-
rational summa. But reversing the strict chronological sequence,
Wright is the Ockham to Le Corbusier's Aquinas, or the Hume to
the latter's Descartes; Le Corbusier's radicalism is characteristically
French, and his dogmatic faith in a cluster of precepts allows him
to demand a comprehensive urbanistic reformation as the necessary
precondition of elementary architectural achievement. It was to
be "Architecture or Revolution." Either the one or the other. Or
sometimes both. But the word *revolution* since 1776 in America and
1789 in France has been impregnated with a very different content.
The one is a kind of legalistic Ark of the Covenant, a stable point of
reference, a political criterion. The other has all the overtones of
1848 and the barricades. It is an assumed principle of social change.
The American supposes the *res publica* to be relatively static, the *res
privata* to be in flux. And, if like all generalisations these are imperfect, the shred of truth that adheres to them permits us to approach
that largely private quality of Wright's achievement and that
largely public demand that penetrates Le Corbusier's.

To be very frivolous, Le Corbusier is the Fourteenth of July
brought up to date. The architectural ancien régime is to take a fall.
A reign of virtue is to be introduced. But Wright was never
equipped with so convenient a *Bastille*—and though he can sometimes sound far too like a Fourth of July orator—his revolution was
conceived of as more of an internal, less of an external event. He is
addressing no constituent assembly. He has little hope of persuad-

ing a Caesar. He is concerned with rendering unto the self. Less politically naive than Le Corbusier, less inflamed by the possibility of any single great redirection of affairs, Wright is the Protestant preoccupation with states of mind rather than with states of order, with experience rather than speculation. On architecture's behalf he anticipates no grand legislative act. By such intervention his libertarian instincts would be affronted. For him amelioration—if it is to come—is to be a process issuing from the individual conscience rather than from any corporate entity.

One may see the virtues and the defects of either point of view. They may both be coercive; but it is in that both may impose intolerable strain, a tension that seeks relaxation in the ordering of a building's *matériel,* that both have been productive of great architecture. Implicitly Le Corbusier overestimates the state, expects it to do what it can never perform. Implicitly Wright places too exalted a premium on the social atom, hopes for a regeneration of which there is no reason to expect that it is capable. And just as any publication by Le Corbusier can madden while it instructs and diverts, so Wright's last book, denominated with characteristic excess *A Testament,* stimulates with its vigor and slightly depresses with the blindness of its conviction.

Wright was a master of words. He was an aphorist, a raconteur, a wit, and a rhetorician; but he preferred simplicity to dialectic, spirit to form; and, professing to distrust logical deduction, the pride of intellect, conventional culture, his repertory of heroes is always apt to be promiscuous and exotic. And thus one may understand when he condemns "anti-formalism in art" and proclaims: "Different were the orientals and different were Jesus, Shakespeare, Milton, Blake, Wordsworth, Coleridge, Keats, Shelley, Beethoven, Bach, Brunelleschi, Goethe, Rembrandt, Dante, Cervantes, Giotto, Mantegna, Leonardo, and Michelangelo. Different were the prophets of the human soul. All Masters of the Nature of Man and the hosts they have inspired."

While one may understand this—partly the result of a pure exuberance of discourse, partly the result of profound cultural intuition—many of Wright's imitators have certainly failed to grasp his full mental range. He was inordinately aware of the natural basis of all genuine classicism. He understood, and perhaps no one better understood, the Romantic insistence that authentic perception is only to be induced by the stimulus of shock. He perfectly apprehended the Burkean and nineteenth century realisation that society is a continuum, an evolving organism, rather than a contract or a construct of political theory. But it is at this stage that we move towards Wright's central act of dissent. He did not see—he preferred to ignore—that the United States is both. He did not see that the image of Washington, thin though it may often be, is a symbol which celebrates the state as a juristic contrivance, that it is the exhibition of a series of propositions demonstrable at law, that this image of equitable regulation is at least as valid for society as for the individual, as is the evocation of life taking nourishment from the soil, spreading itself out to probe the environment, to inhale the elements. For, somewhere in his being, Wright was intensely sympathetic to the ideas of growth and change implicit in English constitutional practice. The image of Westminster, that moving silhouette, that accumulation of expediencies, that most copious of accidents, was something toward which he responded. But just as in America he demanded liberty and required that it be stripped of the carapace of legalities in which it was necessarily enclosed, so if we imagine him in England, that elaborate deference to precedent, that convenient respect for authority would have incited his impatience.

Wright's plastic achievement cannot and should not be separated from his ideas. These are their outward and visible form. But it is on the rock of society that his philosophical boat, like Le Corbusier's, also splits. He can accommodate the individual. He can comprehend all the variousness of private life. But scarcely with his conscious mind is he able to tolerate either the traditional sanctions or the legal fictions with which great political orders ensure their stable continuity. But since this disability is far from being a personal defect of Wright's, or indeed Le Corbusier's, it will be as well

Review: *A Testament*

to pass over it and to deploy attention, not to the possible social consequences of Wright's principles if they were to be applied *in extenso* but rather to their purely formal outcome.

Review: *Architecture: Nineteenth and Twentieth Centuries* by Henry-Russell Hitchcock

Prepared as a script for the BBC, 1958

This review of Henry-Russell Hitchcock's book derives from the same origins as the review of Frank Lloyd Wright's A Testament, *and, once again, it rendered the editorial decision-makers at the BBC much less than overjoyed. But, this time, I was at something of a loss to understand why. This time it could scarcely have been considered too extravagant; on the other hand, was it to be interpreted as insufficiently Marxist and 'party line?'*

But, of course, it is ingenuous on my part even to ask the question. At that time, at the BBC, certain persons had a point of view and were unwilling to tolerate the ventilation of any other—and critical suppression can take on a whole variety of forms.

However, not to worry, since, in retrieving this piece from a box of old papers, I was diverted to discover, for better or worse, that most of the critical motifs (and much of the language) developed in my recent book The Architecture of Good Intentions *were already present here.*

Whenever we attempt to come to an understanding of Modern architecture we are confronted with a series of problems as perplexing as they are contradictory. We might wish to define it, to state its principles, to say what it is. And we find ourselves unable to do so. We find in fact that all we can do is to state what it has been, to describe all the different forms it assumed before it became that thing which we feel it to be today and which presumably it will cease to be tomorrow. Perhaps this is to be expected, for it is a problem not unlike that which is experienced in many other branches of contemporary knowledge; but there issues from it in this case a most curious paradox: that Modern architecture, a movement advertising its relations with the present and with the future, a movement which has always been conscientiously opposed to any overt historicism, that this movement has consistently presented itself through the medium of historical studies.

It scarcely matters that these historical studies have often been of the slightest; it is simply enough to notice that the publicists of Modern architecture have preferred, on the whole, to adopt an historical apologia for their subject; and that typically they have made a presentation of it by providing an account of social change, of technological and aesthetic developments within the last two hundred years.

Thus one might believe that an historical account of perhaps the last two hundred years is in some way vital to the understanding of Modern architecture and that it provides a justification for contemporary stylistic manifestations; and for these reasons Henry-Russell Hitchcock's *Architecture: Nineteenth and Twentieth Centuries* cannot fail to be of extreme significance. For, although not a history of Modern architecture, Professor Hitchcock's book is obviously a study of just that particular tract of time which has been used again and again to throw into relief the virtues of the present day.

Professor Hitchcock himself should scarcely require introduction. The author of a major history of early Victorian architecture, of a standard monograph on Richardson and of another on

Wright, the most tireless connoisseur of nineteenth century building in all its bewildering variety, one of the most eminent American critics of contemporary architecture, Professor Hitchcock is able to survey the European scene with a certain trans-Atlantic calm while he can also approach the American picture with a degree of cosmopolitan detachment. He has been described by no less a judge than Erwin Panofsky as bringing to the study of present-day phenomena "the same respect for historical method and concern for meticulous documentation as are required of a study of fourteenth century ivories or fifteenth century prints"; and, allowing for all this, it was surely to be expected that his contribution to the Pelican History of Art would be exemplary. Nor is it surprising that he has given us the most comprehensive account of architectural development since 1800 which is at present available.

His book has been variously received. Sir John Summerson has pronounced it to be a masterpiece. Mr. John Betjeman has found it good but dull. Sir John Summerson's judgement, I feel, is almost right; but Mr. Betjeman's sentiments, I cannot help thinking, will be widely entertained. *Architecture: Nineteenth and Twentieth Centuries* is not easy to read; and yet, to my mind, it is the reverse of anything dull. Its texture is thick. Its details are intricate. Its episodes are profuse. Its surface is complicated. Its manner is deliberately pedestrian. Reading it, one may well feel weighed down with an unbearable sense of oppression. But, on the other hand, one may also experience something of this same unbearable sense of oppression in the presence of many very great works of art; and although this particular history is not perhaps a very great work of art, still it does exert a similar cathartic effect. It is, we might say, a Gothic book, and reading it, we might feel ourselves to be inside some strange medieval building where an excess of detail requires that everything should be seen in close focus and where, in consequence, we are in no way permitted to discriminate the general structure. We are somewhat baffled as to how or why the mechanism holds together or indeed whether it does. Our appetite is both excited and frustrated by the multiplication of parts none of which seem to offer any key to the external configuration of the whole; so that it is only when, with relief, we detach ourselves from the labyrinth that the firm and entirely clear lines of its general profile begin to emerge. Thus one has a primary and then a delayed reaction to Hitchcock's book. At first, it seems a catastrophe. At last it seems almost a triumph.

Architecture: Nineteenth and Twentieth Centuries rises so very superior to all other attempts to cover the same ground that one is left wondering with what criteria it might be interpreted. To many readers a comparison with Sigfried Giedion's *Space, Time and Architecture* will almost automatically suggest itself, though to me, a reference back to Hitchcock's own little study of 1929 seemed in the first case to be the more appropriate.

Exactly thirty years ago in his *Modern Architecture: Romanticism and Reintegration* Professor Hitchcock provided a remarkably penetrating account of the new architecture which had appeared in the twenties. He had been stimulated by his experience as a student in Paris; he had become convinced of the justice of the architectural revolution which was taking place there and in Germany; he had attempted to elucidate its antecedents; and in doing so, in combining the roles of partisan and historian, he was able to establish a standard of judgement which has permitted many of his conclusions to survive the last three decades without impediment.

Thus in many ways the new book is simply a filling out of the old—almost in the same way that the architecture of the fifties is often a filling out of that of the twenties; and now, as in 1929, Hitchcock is still able to open with extensive discussions of early nineteenth century classicism in Paris and Berlin, in St. Petersburg, Munich, and London. He is still able to give a substantially similar account of the Picturesque and the medieval revival to which it lead. He is able to provide a similar narrative of engineering developments and new building techniques. And he is still able to terminate this first phase in an historical watershed located around 1850.

But thirty years ago the next period, 1850–1890, was left almost entirely neglected; and it is here, as a bridging of this former break, that the most brilliant historical constructions have now been inserted. Prolonged accounts of Second Empire architecture are followed by elaborate analyses of High Victorian Gothic in England; there are further appraisals of Norman Shaw, of his American equivalent H. H. Richardson, and of their contemporaries; while there are two immensely important chapters on the rise of commercial architecture in England and America and of the parallel development of the detached house in both countries.

The general emphasis of this second section then is heavily Anglo-American; and it is this rise into prominence of Anglo-American themes which most clearly distinguishes this book from its predecessor. In 1929 Hitchcock took his stand upon the European Modern movement and the possibilities of order which it seemed to offer. He was anxious to make his compatriots aware of foreign novelties; and he wrote to celebrate the achievements of Le Corbusier, of Oud, of Gropius, and of Mies van der Rohe. But today, apparently, he can feel no such single commitment. He can no longer express himself in unqualified terms about the architects whom thirty years ago he called 'the new pioneers'. For all his judgements have been crossed by a reasonable doubt; and so one might suspect that he begins to consider the European revolution of the twenties to have been what Gian Carlo de Carlo calls "a dandy's revolution: very loud but at the same time respectful of the established order."

At least there is something of this effect produced; and Hitchcock, I think, has been lead to produce it, perhaps against his will, by reason of his admiration for Frank Lloyd Wright. In 1929 he had felt quite justified in excluding Wright's buildings from the canon of Modern architecture and assigning them to a category which he called the 'new tradition'. The 'new tradition' was conceived to be a pre-Modern or a proto-Modern architecture which had enjoyed a heyday somewhat before 1914; and the new traditionalists, members of a generation born in or about the 1860s, were characterised as innovators who could not completely detach themselves from a derivative aesthetic. Along with Wright, they in-

Review: *Architecture: Nineteenth and Twentieth Centuries*

cluded such figures as Berlage and Behrens, Mackintosh and Perret, Hoffmann, Horta and van de Velde.

As the most active, the most voluble and the last surviving member of his generation, Wright, as is well known, objected to being relegated to the role of precursor; and very shortly Hitchcock was compelled to feel that he had made his definition of Western architecture altogether too restrictive. For, as he states elsewhere, if such buildings as Perret's Notre Dame at Raincy and Wright's Johnson Wax Building at Racine, Wisconsin, are not to be considered prime examples of Modern architecture, then the word *Modern* has no meaning.

This little critical about-face provides the most revealing shift of emphasis in the entire book. It obliges Hitchcock to split open the category of 'the new tradition' and to take some of its representatives into "the first generation of modern architects"; and it has further the effect of building up the Anglo-American nineteenth century at the expense of the European twentieth. For the architectural laissez-faire of the Victorians which has been so magnificently sustained by Wright now becomes as crucial an episode as the architectural system making of the great figures who emerged in the Twenties.

The two chapters on commercial and domestic architecture in Great Britain and the United States perhaps more than any other imply this concealed thesis. These two building types, the detached house and the office building, both of them originally peculiar to English-speaking societies, are given an entirely justified emphasis. The *cottage ornée* or ornamental villa of the Regency is traced through all the variations it assumed until it reached apotheosis as Frank Lloyd Wright's contribution to the Chicago suburban scene; while the office building, emerging as the masculine component to the suburban villa, is traced from its humble origins in obscure parts of London and New York to its similar ultimate culmination in Chicago. And if Hitchcock were writing a history of ideas, his chapter on the detached house could easily be prefaced with a notice of both the aesthetic (and the political) theory of Edmund Burke;

while his chapter on commercial architecture could just as easily have been opened with a little tribute to the memory of Jeremy Bentham.

In other words, the reevaluation of Wright has forced a re-evaluation of England, for though Hitchcock does not say as much, it is a continuous parallel which he attempts between a Continental rationalism and an Anglo-American empiricism, devoid of program, and yet so strangely subversive of all Continental system.

And the effect of this parallel, of course, is to introduce a double standard; while Hitchcock's catholicity of judgement, by multiplying possible points of view, only leads us to suspect that all our former certainties were simply partial ideas made absolute. Thus, as the profoundly radical quality of the Anglo-American nineteenth century emerges from the narrative, the Continental twentieth century tends to become largely an affair of revolutionary manifestoes, of doctrinaire gestures, of melodramatic attitudes. It becomes the French Revolution as compared to the American—a wonderfully inspiring theatrical set piece which simply inspires other wonderfully inspiring theatrical set pieces.

It is at this stage that one wishes most acutely that Hitchcock had not confined himself too exclusively to a history of architecture; but had been willing to introduce some history of architectural thought, however slight. For while his superb account of stylistic manifestations, running on as it does without reference to ideas, is entirely suited to the elucidation of the Anglo-American tradition, which we are often told makes little reference to ideas itself, one cannot for instance successfully present Le Corbusier in this way. He is inseparable from his ideology; and so surely was the European Modern movement. Perhaps, after all, it was no more than a stylistic manifestation like all the others; but in implying this judgement Hitchcock will certainly disconcert many of his admirers both in England and in the United States, and he does seem to have written a book without a climax—though as I see it now it would be more true to suggest that he has written a book which makes the minimum allowance for the entirely conventional opinions of the Modern architect.

Review: *Architecture: Nineteenth and Twentieth Centuries*

184

The Modern architect, we might suspect, is accustomed to receive from the historian a thrill somewhat equivalent to that which the Victorian reader of novels was accustomed to receive from the contemporary novelist. He is accustomed in other words to expect a happy ending. Plots and subplots are to be resolved; punishments are to be received; rewards distributed; while the hero and heroine (could they be engineering and architecture, or are they architecture and sociology?), tried and proved by experience, are to be settled down to an extended life of infinite fecundity and unabated bliss. Is it in order in a discussion of architecture to introduce a theological concept and to speak of the eschatology of Modern architecture? Or would it be simpler to propose that histories of architectural development since the industrial revolution have usually led up to the present with the inference that the present is the end of history? The idea that some universal change might bring history to an end is of course one of the oldest human hopes. In the new dispensation, politics or the state are to wither away, Utopia is to be installed, and all moral problems are to become problems of social engineering. And the relation of Modern architecture to this millennial theme was at one time evidently very close. There was to be a universal change of form. It was to be the outward and visible sign, both the cause and the effect, of a universal change of heart; and in the new order, with society redeemed, all problems of aesthetics were to become simply problems of technology.

The disappearance of the idea that Modern architecture is going to redeem the world is what most strikingly differentiates Hitchcock's book from earlier treatments of the same period. Obviously Modern architecture is not going to redeem the world. But how important this proposition was.

Sidgwick Avenue

Published in *The Cambridge Review*, 1959

*This is, I believe, the last of the little pieces which I wrote for English
(and Cambridge) consumption in the academic year 1958–1959; and,
in its results, it was almost the most disappointing. As an attempt to
plug in an academic community with absolutely* no *visual sense to the
iconographical realities of architecture, patently it failed, just as, at
that date, it would have failed in Oxford. It was intended to be the
first of three articles which I proposed to write on this particular topic,
but which, since I found resistance to providing illustrations, I was not
able to continue.*

*The last of my articles written for a Cambridge publication, it
was shortly after this that* The Architectural Review *sent me off to
look at La Tourette.*[1]

There are many reasons why persons will unite together to appraise
or condemn a work of architecture; and of these, its capacity or in-

capacity to service definite physical requirements, its merits or de-
merits as a formal configuration, though invariably paraded and
eminently cogent, are likely to be among the least influential. For,
whatever practical or aesthetic virtues we think we apprehend in
the building which occupies our attention, our discernment is
prone to be directed by considerations quite extraneous to its use or
shape. A building insinuates a subliminal argument. We are always
swayed—generally more than we know—by a connotational significance. Our responses, favourable or not, are extensively conditioned by the degree to which the building may serve as a species of
icon for the excitation of those cultural phantasies upon which we
place high *premia*.

Thus a history of architecture could quite well be written
in which buildings functioned as simply the protagonists of unorga-
nized sentiment; and while, as all histories do, it would infallibly
bias its subject matter, it might—as a contribution to a sociology
of form—still aspire to some legitimate, if limited, value. Presumably the historian would demonstrate the circulation of particular
styles in particular social strata; and, since he would exhibit the
extent to which different interest groups, at different levels of
consciousness, identify themselves with different architectural manifestations, his material would be embarrassingly rich. Ephemeral
quarrels, deep cleavages of cultural allegiance, political alignment,
the stamp of religious affiliation, all would be shown as seeking
their plastic corollaries. As a trivial matter, we should see the Prince
of Wales publicizing his rupture with George III by encouraging
Francophile taste. As a more profound event, Venetian classicism of
the late sixteenth century might be construed as a mirror of Venetian resistance to the court of Rome. In a political milieu, the lively
commerce of the second generation Whigs with this same Venetian
classicism would underscore the revolutionary settlement of 1688
and annotate the dynastic issues of the age of Walpole. And in a
more opportunistic area, we might be allowed a glimpse of the Society of Jesus, in its Netherlandish and French provinces, deliberately
cultivating the conservative sentiment of local patriots by a simu-

lated Gothic expression long after anything of this kind had ceased to be patronized by the ruling elites of Paris and Madrid.

Heavily diluted though this history would be, it would serve as an instructive and a quasi-Warburgian compilation. But the same historian, if he could allow himself so grand and synoptic a vision, could possibly bring his readers almost down to the present day. In England of the nineteenth century he could show us the Gothic Revival, originally—in both its cult of the sublime and its feeling for the particular—so Burkean a movement, becoming transfigured, gradually interpenetrated with Tractarian dogma, and at last issuing, fully equipped with the imprimatur of William Morris, as the outward and visible sign of a socialist Utopia-to-be. And while he might hazard a comparable *renversement des alliances* for the parallel classical development—which he might envisage as a figure of republican virtue converted slowly and voluptuously into an emblem of capitalist largesse—this would be a more debatable subject matter, and he would be better advised to press forward into the twentieth century, where, relating the public success of Modern architecture to the public reception of political reform, he could conclude with an interesting epilogue: that, in the United Kingdom and the United States at least, the official recognition of Modern architecture around 1950 was roughly coincident with the fracturing of those attitudes which had seemingly done so much to foster it.

But if our student of the mythologies which are the dynamic of all architectural change were by temperament more of a miniaturist, if he were indisposed to tolerate the slipshod examination of vast historical panoramas or the cursory summarizing of entities so ample as the Venetian republic, no doubt he could retract his gaze from this level of abstraction, confine himself to a humble and a domestic role, and still elicit equally useful conclusions. For a microcosmic field where so much is condensed—like the University of Cambridge—could readily provide the local historian with more than sufficient material. Indeed we might suppose him (in Gibbon's phrase) disposed to undertake "a candid but rational inquiry." He is equally impartial to the seventeenth or twentieth century origin of

Sidgwick Avenue

any monument: he is prone to examine the self-confident splendour of Victorian John's, Caius, or Pembroke; he is able to scrutinize that strange mid-twentieth diffidence which inspires other collegiate bodies to dissimulate their size—and by implication their influence—through presenting themselves to the world as aggregations of cottages; but while he might be anxious to determine the date—perhaps sometime about 1870—when, except for minor alterations in detail, the Cambridge image was presumed to be fixed; and while—led to speculate as to what psychic needs this fixation corresponded—he might even propose to investigate the consequences of the evident tabu into which it congealed; if *such* might be his programme, at this stage we may conveniently leave him, since both he and his less meticulous colleague are at present introduced as simply an initiatory gambit which here may serve as an overture to stimulate movement in the direction of Sidgwick Avenue.

For the sake of polemical efficiency I have introduced this contracted historical survey so as to adumbrate the remoter dimensions of a judgement such as that upon Lady Mitchell Hall. I have tried to demonstrate that architecture is used for purposes of self-identification, that there exists an architectural underworld in which the most strange psychological syndromes are to be found lurking. But in addition to this it is also necessary to assert that architecture, like any other humanistic discipline, can never be more rational than the society in which it finds itself; that at its very base there will always be found, not only stubborn sentiment and floating obsession, but also some solution of those painful epistemological issues with which we are compelled to struggle.

A work of architecture is a collection of bricks, stone, mortar, steel, concrete, timber, glass, tubes, and entrails, which are necessarily distributed according to the principles of certain known statical laws; but the generally received, and surely not erroneous, supposition that all these miscellaneous materials are to be coordinated for the purposes of use and pleasure already brings us to that famous crossroads where 'fact' and 'value' intersect. For, if the laws of statics may be assumed established beyond dispute, the 'laws' of

use and pleasure, as we are well aware, have not as yet been subjected to any Newtonian revolution; and while it is not inconceivable that as certain techniques of investigation arrive at maturity
these 'laws' may be fully ascertained, until that time any determination of architectural problems will derive from unverified, and unverifiable, hypotheses.

This condition of radical uncertainty is the obvious existen-
tial predicament in which any work of architecture finds itself located. But if it has always been so, it has not always seemed so to
be. For at some times faith, at others Plato have occluded the issue;
and because architectural tradition has been heavily impregnated
first with classical and then with positivist thought, Modern architecture itself for long affected to be just a simple determination of
'facts' or alternatively—according to the submission of one of its
most distinguished proponents—it presented itself as simply "the
inevitable logical product of the intellectual, social, and technical
conditions of our age." But even Modern architecture, for all its theoretical purity, was something rather more than the first and distinctly less than the second; while, since it rapidly became a kind of
litmus paper by means of which the congenital Tory could be distinguished from the temperamental Whig, a scientific observer might
always have made the plausible suggestion that the useful animation of the typical Whig-Tory response had really served as the most
perfect of reagents, indicating in the compound the presence of
something that was said not to be there.

However this is to parenthesise. What Modern architecture
felt itself to be will be interesting to the historian, but here it is of
more peripheric relevance. Modern architecture was misinterpreted;
but though its nature was not deliberately dissembled, to correct a
false impression which its more energetic apologists have definitely
broadcast—an impression which now lies buried in the minds of bu-
reaucrats like a seed about to burst into bud—we must insist that
the phenomenon of architecture is no more a natural than it is a scientific one; and that, while the architect's motivations may often
seem arcane, the definitive qualifications of a work of architecture

are never other than simple. The architect is obliged to perform. He cannot arrest his activity. He cannot hopefully await the day when all his problems have become empirically determinable. He is in the position of the theologian or the political philosopher. He is obliged to predetermine certain issues. He is compelled to call up the ghosts of traditional evaluation, myth, or metaphysics; and therefore his work, the work of architecture, is of its very nature essentially, always, and absolutely an ideological construct.

To insist that this is the category of a work of architecture, that it is what it is, is naive but necessary. For clearly for a corporation in the public eye to appear to sponsor ideological constructs is always a serious matter. An individual may do so, whimsically or with conviction, but a public body has a public face; and though the whole history of culture, whether our index to it is architecture or whether it is not, shows nothing but the grandest succession of ideological constructs, we—by which I mean we of average education—are apt to feel them to be rather less than respectable companions; and until they become of certain age, being prone to suspect them not to be "real," we feel obliged to deceive ourselves as to their status. It was probably always so; but, if we have here an innate propensity of the human species, it has clearly been seriously aggravated by the intellectual history of the last two hundred years. For this is a mental development which can never be subtracted from the record; which—though it can have no absolute value and should not be equipped with coercive capacity—can, as a psychic orientation, barely be excised from the consciousness. And, if we know that the thought of the last two hundred years has, for good or ill, called in doubt convention, that it has made unverifiable hypotheses more scandalous than before, that—by discovering the stimulus of shock to be essential to the authenticity of perception—it has made change a *desideratum* in itself, we are also aware that (while it has circumscribed the areas of certainty and thereby the possibility of ethical deportment) it has simultaneously exalted the private, abjured the passive, called for the active, and demanded the public.

This, in the most generalized terms, was the curse of nineteenth century architecture as it was the dilemma of nineteenth century thought; and this dilemma, I cannot think, has really been laid to rest. Rather it is shelved; and we exercise an unerring sense of *raison d'état* by pretending that ideological constructs are something other than what they are. One of the more characteristic tragicomic aspects of the present day, this is never far absent from architectural dispute in which, again and again, we may discover one party trying to pilot an ideological construct by maintaining that such is not its nature and another party attempting to sabotage the same construct by an equal exercise in dissimulation. Nor should this be unexpected. For, in an age in which ideology is generally suspect though its operations are rampant, we are still obliged to build. And we are therefore obliged to sponsor ideological constructs. In other words we are obliged to declare ourselves. And because this is a matter of much acute embarrassment, because a declaration establishes a target at which the hostile may shoot, because a declaration limits choice and therefore seems to confine the future, we are well able to understand the ambivalent situation in which representative public institutions are placed and the diffidence which they characteristically evince.

And we might find *some* reason here—although economic necessity would be considered the more respectable cause—for that positive frenzy (it amounts to nothing else) in the conversion of existing properties, which, since 1945, has gripped the United Kingdom. Let us only here notice that Edwardian government, a relatively feeble institution, housed itself in sumptuous palaces which might have lead the observer to an overestimate of its power; but that we can proceed with incomparably greater caution. So that the modern state, an all-embracing institution, distinguishing liberality from liberalism, is typified by the desire to hide itself and characteristically conceals its bureaucracy in imperfectly revised Georgian terraces, in Palladian houses on the other side of lakes, and in anonymous office buildings which, so that it may inhabit them with the good conscience of neutrality, it has allowed speculators to erect.

These are some of the issues which obfuscate English building today. We will judge them according to our several points of view. But meanwhile, if a building is never less than a symbolic utterance, if it is a hieroglyph which witnesses the situation in which it arose, let us observe that no one approaching Sidgwick Avenue can fail to recognize that this particular hieroglyph is eminently legible. An academic Ville Radieuse, a most portentous symbol of the twentieth century, has been successfully hidden. It is screened: first from Queen's Road by its site, second from Sidgwick Avenue by its wall; and, since it gestures to itself in isolation which is less splendid than complete, we will decipher a debate, a victory, an uncertainty, a frustration, and a decision—that ostentatious celebrations should not be indulged.

But the physical melancholy of that suburban street which leads so inexorably into the prairies of nowhere cannot fail to stimulate further speculation. For, if already we think we discern the circumstances in which Sir Hugh Casson was briefed and begin to believe that they may have contributed a certain color to his design, our suspicion is soon no more than a link in a chain of reflection. A propitiary and a tactful decision was made. A respectable group of buildings has resulted. Elsewhere in the town many outrageous, crude, shapeless, and lumpy structures, displaying no evidence of intellect, decorum, or elementary discretion, have lately appeared. They have not incited enthusiasm. They have not been extensively condemned. They have been tolerated; and one may ask why, when they have been found acceptable, a precedent should now be established by the rejection of a design which at least the knowledgeable consider to be possessed of merit.

Clearly one reason may be that the sense of prerogative is often slow to awaken; that, though members of Regent House have voted to accept the later stages of the Lensfield Road Chemical Laboratories, the Chemical Engineering Building on the New Museums Site, the wings to the Engineering Building, the houses for Physiology and Psychology and for Veterinary Anatomy on the Downing Site, and the earlier stages of the Sidgwick Avenue development, in all these cases they may very well have been unaware that they were empowered with the discretion to refuse. But, if this may be one reason why the decision over Lady Mitchell Hall has established a precedent; and if another may be a growing sensitiveness to architectural manifestations in general; and if we may also suspect that the criterion of judgement become elevated to the degree to which the phenomena judged become adequate; we are also compelled to notice the extravagant singularity of this present judgement. Regent House has always been enabled to accept or reject building contracts, but only once before has it attempted to reject; and this was in the case of the Ministry of Works hut outside the Marshall Library—whose aesthetic offensiveness was ultimately justified by reason of its patriotic necessity.

Thus, while the temper of disapprobation may or may not be consistent, we may well suspect that it rises, becomes hectic, in relation to the presence of stylistic differentiae; that the final issue is neither visual nor utilitarian; that within the overt judgement there is secreted a reaction, not to questions of formal preference or functional performance, but to the cluster of sentiments, ideas, and evaluations which is very imperfectly designated "Modern architecture."

Note

1. See Colin Rowe, "Dominican Monastery of La Tourette, Eveux-sur-Arbresle, Lyon," *Architectural Review* 129, no. 772 (June 1961), later published in *Mathematics of the Ideal Villa and Other Essays* (Cambridge, Mass.: MIT Press, 1976).

Index of Names

Adams, Henry, 172
Albers, Josef, 32, 40
Albini, Franco, 120
Antwerp, 133
Architectural Association, x, 153,
    159–165
Arnaud, Leopold, 111–112
Arnold, Matthew, 168
Austin, A. Everett, 18

Bancroft, George, 13
Banham, Reyner, ix–x
Barnstone, Howard, 22, 132
Barr, Alfred, 18
Bauhaus, 48–50
Bayer, Herbert, 21
Belluschi, Pietro
    Equitable Life Insurance Building
       (Portland), 77–80

Berenson, Bernard, 11, 12, 13
Betjeman, John, 179
Blake, Peter, 116
Borromini, Francesco, 9
    Oratorio dei Filippini (Rome), 9, 10
Breuer, Marcel, 116, 118, 120
British Broadcasting Company, 135,
    167, 177
Brown, Arthur, Jr., 6–10
Brown, Jasmine, 6–10

Cambridge University, 36, 131–132,
    134, 143–151, 187–193
Casson, Hugh, 146, 150, 192
Chicago, 111, 124, 126
Chimacoff, Alan, 37, 39
Cockerell, Charles Robert, 171
Conant, James Bryant, 20
Condet, Neville, 146, 150

Constructivism, 115, 160
Cornell University, 35–37
Cubism, 31, 115, 127, 139–140
Curtis, Nathaniel Cortland, 109, 117

De Stijl, 115, 116, 160
Doesburg, Theo van, 31, 43, 44, 74

Ecole des Beaux-Arts, 8, 10, 48–50,
    108, 111, 113–114
Eisenman, Peter, 35, 42, 131, 134
Emerson, Ralph Waldo, 169
Empson, William, 104
Entenza, John, 25, 38

Garnier, Charles, 171
Gestalt psychology, 100–105
Giedion, Sigfried, 20–21, 180
Gordon, Elizabeth, 29
Gowan, James, 143, 146–149
Gromort, Georges, 8, 9
Gropius, Walter, 20, 50, 74, 114, 116,
    119, 120, 127
    Bauhaus buildings (Dessau), 115
Guadet, Julien, 49, 108–117, 120

Hamlin, Talbot, 107–108, 113–120
Harbeson, John F., 109
Harris, Harwell Hamilton, 28, 30–35,
    37–40, 42
Harris, Jean Murray Bangs, 25–34, 37–
    39, 41, 42, 55
Harvard University, 12–13, 20, 21
Hejduk, John, 32, 35, 39, 43, 55, 132
Hirsche, Lee, 32, 35, 40
Hitchcock, Henry-Russell, 11–22, 43,
    171, 178–184
Hodgden, Lee, 35–37
Hoesli, Bernhard, 27, 30–35, 39–40,
    41–43
House and Garden, 155
House Beautiful, 29

Johnson, Philip, 11, 18, 19
Joyce, James, 97

Kassaboff, George, 142
Kepes, Gyorgy, 75, 80, 97
Key, Sydney, 4–5

Labrouste, Henri, 108
Le Corbusier, 16, 20, 30–32, 43, 109,
    113–114, 116, 119, 127, 135–
    142, 156, 173–174
    Algiers, skyscraper project for,
      75–77
    Garches, villa at, 14, 16–17, 115
    League of Nations project, 120
    Maison Domino, 43, 44, 74, 139
    Pavillon Suisse, 140
    Unité d'Habitation (Marseilles), 160
    Ville Radieuse, 137, 140, 160, 192
Leipziger-Pierce, Hugo, 27, 30, 32
Lewis, Sinclair, 70–71
Lewis, Wyndham, 135–136
London, 134
Lubetkin, Berthold, 142
Lutyens, Edwin, 169–172

Martin, Leslie, 36, 132
Maxwell, Robert, 2
McKim, Mead and White, 123
Meier, Richard, 35
Michelangelo Buonarroti, 137
    project for San Lorenzo (Florence),
      89–97
Mies van der Rohe, Ludwig, 29, 32,
    43, 115, 127
    Barcelona Pavilion, 115
Moholy-Nagy, László, 97
Moholy-Nagy, Sybil, 11
Mondrian, Piet, 74, 94, 115
    Victory Boogie-Woogie, 94–97
Moore, Charles, 73

Morris, William, 187
Mumford, Lewis, 124–129

Norton, Charles Eliot, 13, 169

Olmsted, Frederick Law, 126
Oud, J. J. P., 115

Panofsky, Erwin, 179
Pei, I. M.
    Mile High Center (Denver), 77–83
Perret, Auguste
    Notre-Dame du Raincy, 182
Pevsner, Nikolaus, 11, 74
Pickering, Ernest, 109
Porter, Arthur Kingsley, 12, 13

Rainaldi, Carlo, 8–10
    Santa Maria in Campitelli (Rome), 9,
        10
Richardson, H. H., 170–171
Robertson, Howard, 109
Robertson, Jacquelin, 134
Rome, 4, 8–10
Rossiter, Clinton, 131–132, 134
Rubin, Irwin, 32, 35, 40
Ruskin, John, 13, 111, 169

Saint-Denis, abbey of, 83, 84
Schinkel, Karl Friedrich, 110
Schumacher, Tom, 37, 39
Seligmann, Werner, 35–37
Semper, Gottfried, 110
Shankland, Graeme, 142
Shaw, John, 35–37
Shaw, Norman, 170, 171
Slutzky, Robert, 32, 35, 40, 73–74,
    132
Smith, Peter van der Meulen, 14–16
Smithson, Alison and Peter, 148, 150

Smyth, Craig, 5
Soby, James Thrall, 18
Stein, Gertrude, 55
Stirling, James, 2, 20, 142
    project for Churchill College, Cam-
        bridge (with James Gowan), 143,
        146–149
Sullivan, Louis, 111, 126
Summerson, John, 179

Terragni, Giuseppe, 16, 120
Texas, 26–27, 55–71

United Nations Building, New York,
    75, 77
United States, 5, 10, 55–57, 70–71,
    153–157, 169–170, 173
University of Texas, 26–35, 39, 41–53

Van Pelt, John Vredenburgh, 109
Venice, 83
    Ca' d'Oro, 83–86
    Palazzo Mocenigo, 87–89
Vignola, Jacopo da
    Villa Farnese (Caprarola), 81–83
Viollet-le-Duc, Eugène-Emmanuel,
    110

Whiffen, Jean, 27–28
Whiffen, Marcus, 27–28
Wittkower, Rudolf, 2, 8, 10, 21, 117
Wolfe, Tom, x
Wright, Frank Lloyd, 22, 31, 32, 43,
    127, 167–176, 181–183
    Johnson Wax Administration Build-
        ing (Racine), 182
Wurster, Catherine Bauer, 28
Wurster, William, 28

Yale University, 21–22

Index